BRIDGE 2 DESTRUCTION

The Sequel to Dealt the Wrong Hand

A Novel by

QUEEN B.G.

Published by Top Notch Publishing

All rights reserved. Without limiting the rights under copyright reserved above. No part of this book may be reproduced, stored in or introduced into a retrieval system, or transmitted, in any form, or by any means (electronic, mechanical, photocopying, recording, or otherwise), without prior written consent from both the author, and publisher La' Femme Fatale' Publications, except brief quotes used in reviews. For information regarding special discounts or bulk purchases, please contact Top Notch Publishing

Library of Congress Catalog Card No: In publication data
ISBN: 978-0-9840077-0-7
Copyright: 2011 by Top Notch Publishing
Bridge 2 Destruction
Written by: Queen B
Text Formation: Write on Promotion

This is a work of fiction. It is not meant to depict, portray or represent any particular real person. All the characters, incidents, and dialogues are the products of the author's imagination and are not to be construed as real. Any references or similarities to actual events, entities, real people, living or dead, or to real locales are intended to give the novel a sense of reality. Any similarity in other names, characters, entities, places, and incidents is entirely coincidental. All rights reserved, including the right of reproduction in whole or part in any form.

Published by
Top Notch Publishing

ACKNOWLEDGMENTS

As always, I have to thank God. He is a part of everything I am and everything I do. I'm grateful for all of his blessings and most of all for his faithfulness to me.

To my kids: I love all of you and I appreciate all of your patience and understanding. All of this is for you!

To Manson, the love of my life: This has been one helluva ride! Thank you for your support, love, and patience because without it I don't know how I would've done it. You mean the world to me and I pray that you see it *Muah*

I absolutely have to thank (my stuster) Niccole and my girl Ni'cola Mitchell, you two are the best. Whenever I need either of you, you are always there and I LOVE YOU for that. Cali Connect, you guys are the best support team ever. We have our times but at the end of the day we know it's all out of love.

Lastly, I want to shout out all of my family, friends, readers, supporters, etc. I absolutely love and appreciate all of you. Continue to support my dream and I'll continue to produce the best quality of work imaginable. For everyone associated with this project, I appreciate you. It's full speed ahead from here…..LET'S GO!!!

~The Shooting Star

Dedication

I would like to dedicate this project to myself. I'm doing this for many different reasons. My journey as an author has been rough and somewhat of a heartache but through it all I managed to push through everything and everyone that stood in my way. At one point it caused me to question whether or not this was gonna happen for me. After a long conversation with God I learned to let go of everything that was wrong and fight toward everything I knew was right. Now here I am... I'm self-publishing my second book, CEO of my own company with authors under my umbrella, and successful in it all. I love the fight in me because that fight + God has gotten me through everything.

BRIDGE 2 DESTRUCTION

The Sequel to Dealt the Wrong Hand

Chapter One

"KeKe! What you doing?"

With my gun held tightly in my hand I turned to identify yet another soon to be victim. Bianca, an eight-year-old little girl who was also the daughter of one of my clients in the dope game, had seen everything. She stood there full of innocence with a look of confusion on her face. All I could wonder was; *how much had she seen? What should I do?* And the harsh reality of the situation hit me like a cold-hearted slap in the face. No witnesses can be left behind.

Fuck! Now I'm gone have to kill this little bitch, I thought to myself. Bianca and I stared into each others eyes and what I saw before me, sent me into a daze. This was an innocent little girl with her whole life ahead of her. There's no telling what the future may hold for her. In truth, I was starring at a reflection of me. I was this little girl. A positive future ahead of me, a crack addicted mother, and nothing but negativity surrounding me; waiting, destroying, and manipulating everything I was destined to be. I really don't wanna kill this little girl but I can't risk being fingered for this murder. In the same token, a child killer wasn't something I was and I definitely wasn't interested in becoming one. In all honesty any person who killed a child and had anything to do with me, would suffer some extreme consequences.

Kai sat in the car screaming with frustration, "Come on Cuz, we gotta go! What-the-fuck-man-damn!"

But everything had stopped. I couldn't move and didn't hear a word she was sayin'. My thoughts were the only thing I was able to grasp at that moment. As soon as I was like, fuck it, gunplay erupted breaking my trance and bringing me back to reality.

BOOM! BOOM! BOOM!

POW! POW! POW!

In the midst of my daze one of Mouse's folks emerged from the back of the building taking clear shots at me and Kai was returning fire. My first reaction was to grab Bianca but it was too late. Everything had happened so fast. Bianca's body hit the pavement in silence from being struck in the chest by one of the bullets. The mixed emotions I felt a few short seconds ago were all for nothing because despite my decision to let her live, Bianca was killed anyway. Fire built up in my eyes and an indescribable pain twisted in my heart. With murder on my mind I moved cautiously toward my enemy rapidly releasing bullet after bullet in his direction.

"Ugh!" One of my bullets connected hitting my enemy in his torso causing him to back away and try to seek shelter from yet another possible bullet wound. With three shots left I managed to tear a hole through his left thigh and his left shoulder. My mission was to kill him and I wasn't backing down until I did so. But the squeeze of the trigger gave off a clicking sound indicating I was fresh out of ammunition. My only option now was to make it to the car. Fortunately, I made it, but not before being hit in the arm by one of his bullets.

"Fuck! Go Kai, go!" I yelled while grabbing my arm.

Kai screeched off down the street in an attempt to make a clean getaway. As she drove back to the hood I took off my sweater to get a better look at the damage done to my arm. It burned like hell and I was bleeding ridiculously but the bullet had only grazed me. My arm had a big gash in it like someone tried to cut a big chunk out of my arm with a butcher knife. The pain was nothing compared to what I was feeling for Bianca. The moment her little body hit the pavement I completely grew cold and had made up my mind that the unfamiliar man had to die and it had to be as soon as possible. When she was killed a part of me died with her. I would give anything to get that moment back.

"Fuck KeKe!" Kai yelled as she maneuvered through the streets.

"Kai, Cuz, that little girl is dead man. I can't believe this shit. I got to kill this nigga. He doesn't deserve to see another second."

"What if I killed her?" Kai asked softly, looking at me through saddened eyes, thinking to herself how fucked up it would be if she found out her bullet was the bullet that killed the little girl.

"Damn you're right. I don't think so though."

"Why not? You can't say that because we were both shooting," Kai said while shaking her head in disbelief, looking at me then back to the road. She suddenly became quiet and drifted off into deep thought. My aim is always on point though so hopefully it was him and not me. *I can't live wit this shit*, she thought to herself.

After making it safely to the hood we jumped in my car and drove to Gardena for NeNe to work her magic. Though it wasn't all that bad I definitely needed stitches and under these circumstances I wasn't going to the hospital. It took us all of ten minutes to get to Nene's house and that whole ten minutes was spent arguing back and forth about Bianca. We were angry and heartbroken over the situation but now wasn't a good time for any of this. The last thing we needed was for NeNe to find out. She knew we were coming so when we pulled up she opened the garage door for us to park. As we pulled in the garage we both dried the tears from our eyes as discreetly as possible. Entering the house NeNe asked, "KeKe what the hell are you doing? You see what I'm left wit' and you gone be much worse if you continue to do what you are doing."

Damn, I thought to myself. *Does this bitch already know the business?* Not sure of the reasoning behind her statement I remained nonchalant and replied, "I hear you NeNe but it is what it is. Can you please just hook me up so we can get goin'?"

"You can get mad if you want to KeKe but I'm telling you what I know. I expect this type of shit from these niggas but you? You too smart and way too pretty to end up in jail for life or laid out dead somewhere."

Moments later things heated up causing NeNe, along with many other Los Angeles residences, to lose their minds.

"And now for some breaking news," we heard a voice coming from the television sitting just across the room causing Kai and I to become fully alert. NeNe stood in silence also as we all focused our attention on the television. "We are live here in South Los Angeles where neighbors reported a shooting this afternoon. Police are investigating the shooting of a black male in his late thirties and the unfortunate death of an eight-year-old little girl whose name has not yet been released. Witnesses say that at least two suspects were involved in the shooting and reported seeing a black mid-sized car fleeing the scene. 77th Street Division will be working overtime on this investigation to ensure the family of this precious little girl find justice. Reporting from South Los Angeles this is..."

NeNe shook her head stating, "Now that's sad." The looks on our faces must have sent off bad signals because she looked at the two of us and went stone retarded on us.

"You got to be kidding me. A kid! KeKe did you do this?"

"Hell naw I didn't! I swear to god I didn't kill that little girl."

Kai sat silently looking sad and confused. When she dropped her head into the palm of her hands NeNe knew something was wrong.

"Kai!"

Kai said nothing. She didn't even lift her head. She sat silently sobbing wanting this to all be over like a bad dream.

"Kai!" NeNe repeated this time walking in her direction and snatching Kai's arm away from her face. "Did you do this?"

Kai burst out in tears, "I don't know man. If I did, I swear to God I didn't mean to. I'm not no child killer!"

With that said NeNe embraced her and tried to console her the best she could. While she was compassionate toward Kai, she went hard on me. After releasing Kai from her arms NeNe approached me like she was about to take off or somethin'. "KeKe, I should beat yo' ass. You supposed to be setting an example for your sister and look what you done got her caught up in."

There was nothing I could say because in my heart I knew she was right. Stuck in that moment not knowing what to do I sat down and let NeNe get some things off her chest. NeNe was on me tough. I knew it was all out of love but I wasn't in the mood for none of that shit. While she cleaned me up and put the seven stitches in my arm she continued with her lecture. Even Kai had gotten agitated though. We didn't need to hear this shit right now. Everything NeNe said began to go through one ear and out the other. By the time she was done with her speech my arm was bandaged up and I headed to the car with Kai right behind me.

"Alright NeNe, I love you my nigga. Thanks for hookin' me up," I said and gave her a hug along with one hundred and fifty dollars.

"KeKe did yo' ass listen to anything I just said?"

"Yeah Cuz, I heard you alright."

BRIDGE 2 DESTRUCTION

As we exited the house NeNe stood shaking her head in disappointment with her arms crossed.

~$~

Two days until my brother's funeral and I hadn't even decided what I was gonna wear. Shit the way I'm feelin' I wouldn't give a fuck what I wore. My mind and my focus were still on my brother not being here with me. And the fact that Bianca's funeral would soon be approaching wasn't helpin' none either. At this moment all I could think about was how much my brother loved me and how tight we were. There wasn't nothin' we didn't do together, nowhere had we gone without each other and no one who could fuck with one of us and not see some gangsta shit result from the other one. At times, he thought he was my daddy. He was so overprotective I was afraid of bringing my male friends around him. He would beat their asses for even thinking they could fuck with me. And although I hated when he did that to me, to settle the score I would do the same to all of his female friends. Memories like these are what were tough to deal with. However they were all I had left. No one in this world would amount to him. He had qualities that were hard to find in one individual; loyalty was his main thing, he had jokes like a muthafucka, hands that were deadly, was always sober, and crazy as hell. If you asked me I think he qualified for three SSI checks a month. Who else, other than a crazy person, would play chicken with an ambulance in full pursuit on a fuckin' bike? Every time he did shit like that it scared the shit outta me but he wasn't the least bit scared. Instead, it gave him some type of an adrenaline rush.

When it came to fighting my nigga was a beast. He loved it and craved it on a daily basis. In the hood, meetings were mandatory and you must be on time. He would go to every hood meeting late just to see who was gonna discipline him that day. That was a joke within itself because the discipliners would always end up fucked up as if they were the ones who did somethin' wrong. Damn I miss my brother.

"KeKe you okay?" Kai asked while resting her hand on my shoulder.

"Yeah I'm good. Just thinkin' bout my nigga, ya know? The good times of course."

BRIDGE 2 DESTRUCTION

Sensing my overwhelming sadness, Kai smiled and chuckled sayin', "You remember when we heard all of those gun shots and a car burning rubber in front of the house bumpin' music real loud...."

"Yeah," I said to her forcing a smile on my face. "And his dumb ass came in eatin' some skittles talking' bout, what?" The nigga act like he was wit' the business so I tested the water. "What? Why you lookin at me like that?" I said finishing her statement while imitating my brother. He was smiling big and knew he was wrong. Kai and I laughed in unison.

"Just ignorant as hell for no reason at all," I said to her still laughing.

It felt good to laugh. For the first time since it happened I found the strength to smile. Even Kai enjoyed a smile or two. And that alone was enough to motivate me to go shopping for the funeral. The four of us, Kai, Niece, Lea and I, had gone together so no one would be rushing tomorrow to find something at the last minute. My sisters had awakened something in me that had been unconscious for days. I wasn't happy but my mind was on something other than killing people for a change. The numbness caused by the loss of my brother had now become a slight tingling sensation and with time, I'm sure with time, I'll regain control of my actions. But when, I'd never know.

Kai's depression had even faded away for the moment. With the death of Bianca weighing heavy on her heart it was good to see her smiling for a change. For the past two days, since the incident occurred she was beginning to slip deeper and deeper into a depression. She wouldn't eat, couldn't sleep, and wouldn't get out of bed to take a shower even if you paid her to. Today was different. All it took was a shoulder to lean on and some comforting words on the situation and she began to come around. Hearing the update of the investigation on the news helped a great deal too.

"Officers have now released the name of the victim killed in the South Los Angeles shooting just days ago. The victim is said to be eight-year-old Bianca Taylor." A photo of Bianca wearing a multi-colored, flower sun dress holding her hands together and pressed softly against her face, smiling, looking precious as could be, appeared on the television screen. *"Officers*

say that, Keontay Bridges, the thirty-eight-year-old male also shot at the scene has been placed in custody in connection with the murder. Evidence found at the scene suggests that he was a shooter in the incident that occurred that afternoon. Bridges is currently being held in Los Angeles County Detention Center with no bail. We'll keep you updated as the investigation continues."

That particular news broadcast didn't totally solve the paranoia Kai was experiencing but it did however; give her a sense of relief, knowing that he was in custody for it. Today was definitely going to be a good day.

~$~

My sisters and I spent the rest of the day shopping and getting our hair done. While getting our hair done Kai and I rehearsed a song we were supposed to sing at the funeral. Mariah Carey's, *Hero* was the perfect song and Kai and I were gonna make it a duet. The closer it had gotten to the funeral the more I began to feel like I wasn't gonna be able to do it. Kai tried to convince me otherwise but today even she felt that way. At the end of the day we decided we would just sing it for the family at the dinner tonight and let someone else sing at the funeral. With that decision made, I wrote a poem and if push came to shove Big Chocolate could read it for me.

~$~

"So when you feel like hope is gone / look inside you and be strong / and you'll finally see the truth / that a he-ro lies innnn..... Yooou!"

The family loved it. They clapped, hugged and kissed us, and tears flowed down their faces. "I love you KeKe! *Umm-wuah*," his mom said kissing the dampness of my cheek as tears flowed down my face.

"Thank you Kai! I love you baby!" she said to Kai and kissing her the same.

"Y'all have to sing this tomorrow. For real y'all that is so beautiful."

As much as we wanted to and knew that what she said was true, it wasn't gonna work. I knew that once I walked into that church my emotions were gonna get the best of me. So despite my want to go through with this I gave my final decision which was, "No! I can't." They understood where I was coming from and just embraced me showing their appreciation for us at least sharing that special tribute with the family.

After packing up and saying good-bye, I decided to pay Bianca's family a visit to extend my condolences to them. The whole ride there I thought about what I would say and nothing in particular came to mind. Driving through the empty, late-night streets allowed me to make it there with the quickness. As I approached the door I scanned my surroundings and got sick to my stomach. The yard was nasty lookin' and smelled like dogs shitted here all day, every day. When I knocked on the wooden door, Charmaine, Bianca's mother, appeared in the doorway lookin' a hot mess.

"Can I help you?"

Charmaine looked at me as if I was a stranger and I replied, "Can I come in please? I need to holla at you."

"KeKe? Girl I'm sorry I didn't know that was you," she said opening the door and giving me a hug. Usually I wouldn't have let her get close to me like that but I understood she needed it right now. Regardless of what she's doin' and how bad it's gotten Bianca was her child. I can only imagine the pain she must be feelin' right now.

"KeKe, this is my mom, Freda."

"Nice to meet you Freda," I said giving her a hug also. "My sincere condolences, to you and your family for your loss."

"Thanks baby," she said with sad, watery eyes and a handkerchief held tightly in her right hand.

"I can't stay long so I'm gonna get straight down to business. The reason I came over here is because I've known Charmaine for quite some time now and Bianca was special to me. I know that nothing can ever replace her or erase the pain you all must be feelin' right now, but I *can* make it easier. To take some of the weight off of you guy's shoulders I am willing to pay for the funeral."

Charmaine's eyes grew big as she took in the good news and her mother Freda just cried and fell to her knees thanking God for this wonderful blessing.

Seeing her rejoice in such a way caused tears to build up in my eyes. My heart was in the right place and I felt like my actions were greatly appreciated.

"Here is nine thousand dollars," I said sliding Freda an envelope sealed with Bianca's name on it. "This should be enough to cover a beautiful ceremony. I'm giving it to you because I know it's in good hands. If you ever need me for anything," I said looking into Charmaine's eyes with a sincere facial expression written on my face, "you call me." Again, she hugged me and sobbed on my shoulder thanking me repeatedly for what I had done. While walking out the door she whispered to me, "I'm gonna get my life right KeKe. I promise. As soon as I do, I'm gonna look out for you the way you looked out for me."

A smile spread across my face and I replied, "You don't owe me anything. If you gon' get yourself together do it for you, better yet, do it for Bianca."

As I walked down the walkway and jumped in my car, Charmaine stood in the doorway accompanied by her mother and waved good-bye.

~$~

The next morning we drove to the church in silence. There were no words, no tears, nothing exchanged. Maybe the four of us were all trying to grasp the whole reality of the current event. Or maybe, just maybe, we were all trying with all our might to be as strong as our brother would want us to be. Either way, here we were and it was time to enter the church that would mark the last place we'd ever see his face, the last place we'd ever be able to look at him and tell him how we feel. As the doors of the car swung open my heart began to clinch. People from all walks of life were in attendance watching as we exited the car. When my feet hit the asphalt my mind started working overtime trying to remind me that I could do this. Once out the car my sisters and I entered the church hand in hand. The onlookers watched as the four of us went to face our fear with strength in our walk, our head held high and our appearance top-notch-fly. Unbeknownst to them, behind this fly gear, these glasses, and this strong stride I was crumbling to little pieces. A big lump had developed in my throat, my heart was beating fast, and my hands were shaking with rage. That voice that was just loudly repeating itself, *You can do this*, was now a faint whisper. And as soon as they played that first song

I cracked. I was no longer able to be strong or pretend this wasn't happening. I cried profusely while family members and friends tried to console me. Their words meant nothing to me especially since I couldn't hear them. They hugged me and caressed my back but still it did nothing.

Big Chocolate came over to me and grabbed me by the hand in an attempt to take me outside. My legs wouldn't move. I was weak. With all of her strength she lifted me to my feet and held me close as she guided me down the aisle and out the double doors.

"KeKe! Listen to me Cuz. You stronger than this. This is fucked up man, I know, but he wouldn't want you to be like this. You know his ass would be talking shit tellin' you to suck that shit up."

Choc was right. And with that said I wiped my face and tried to pull myself together. After about five minutes or so Choc asked, "You ready?"

"Yeah but Choc…" my voice was soft and jittery, "Can you read this poem for me cuz I don't think I can do it."

"I'll go up there with you. If you still can't read it then, yeah, I'll do it."

She wrapped me in her arms and told me she loved me and the two of us walked back in the church. I was cool after that and when it was time to read the poem Choc was right there next to me just like she promised. I don't know if it was her supporting me or if it was just me needing to get this off my chest but I read it by myself. Due to my nervousness and my sudden urge to cry, I fucked up towards the end, but it was okay. My brother got the message and so did everyone who sat within these church walls. Up until they started the viewing I held shit together pretty good. When I walked up to that casket and saw him lying there I snapped. He was really gone. Everything started to flash before me like a fucked up movie. I couldn't help but think this was my fault. I left him that night after he told me not to. I knew it was some shit earlier that evening but I thought nothing of it. And I can't ignore the fact that this is my brother. Nobody was gon' ride with him the way I was; and had I been there this wouldn't have happened. I lost it and so did my sisters. They flipped out as if my inner emotions were identical to theirs, causing the same exact reaction. My mind was made up. After the funeral somebody was gon' die.

Chapter Two

The drive to the cemetery was the complete opposite of the drive to the church. Songs were being played in memory of him, emotions were blaring, and a lot of violent promises were made. The funeral procession was so long that it took seven motorcycle escorts to help guide the many attendees to the burial site. Blue rags could be seen flying in the wind as gang members from various hoods performed acts of respect for my brother. As we neared the cemetery entrance police surfaced out of nowhere. No one knew why they had come or where they were coming from but would soon find out. Driving in front of me was my new boyfriend Matt also known on the streets as Lil P. Matt and I had gotten together after TG failed to get his shit together. He was tall, dark and handsome with a gorgeous smile and long hair that was usually braided in two braids hanging neatly over his shoulders, ending at his rib cage. The police were closing in on him so I pulled up on his bumper as close as I possibly could to prevent them from getting behind him. That didn't work; they pulled his ass over anyway and snatched him out of his Cadillac truck slammin' him down on the hot asphalt. *What the fuck*, I thought to myself while unbuckling my seat belt. One of the officers quickly elbowed him in the head causing me to immediately jump out of my car and go ballistic.

"What the fuck are y'all doing? We on our way to a burial and y'all just swoop up breaking up the funeral procession, for what?"

"Back up ma'am and let us do our job," this little dorky ass white cop walked up on me sayin', with one hand pointed in my direction and the other on his waist band.

"Fuck yo' job! This is some disrespectful shit. What y'all pull him over for?"

I was irritated as hell and today was the wrong day to pull this type of stunt. Muthafuckas were drunk, emotional, and completely irrational. Before long everyone had emerged from their vehicles and started to go off. The way they emerged from their vehicles resembled a swat team on a mission to capture their dangerous suspect. It wasn't until now that I noticed the police had pulled over every Cadillac truck in the funeral procession driven by males. All of them were slammed faced down on the ground and treated aggressively.

"Cuz, get the fuck off of me!" one of the guys yelled after being slammed up against the patrol car by a big, corn-fed lookin' ass officer. The interior of their vehicles were destroyed while they searched high and low for anything they could find. Door panels were pulled apart, seats were detached, and the lining in the trunk area was pulled up. With the emotions from the death of our loved one and the anger from the police disrespecting the funeral and destroying folk's property, mayhem began. The police should have seen it comin' but their dumb asses didn't. Once the first group of protesters rallied up against them in an attempt to challenge their authority, reality should have set in. Another officer approached me after jumping off of his motorcycle, talking to me like slavery days were still in effect. "Hey you little Miata," which I know means monkey in Spanish. "Back up and put your fucking hands up," he said pointing at me.

"Who in the fuck are you talking to? You got me fucked up. And you better get yo finger outta my face."

"Shut up and put your hands up," he repeated. When I wouldn't back down or comply with his orders he pepper sprayed me and my natural reflexes caused me to react. Within seconds I threw a jab that connected with his jaw and kept on swingin'. Luckily for me, his aim was off when he pepper sprayed me so I was still able to see. However, the whole left side of my face was burning like hell like someone had ignited a flame on my face. Needless to say, all that did was cause me to flip out even more.

One after another my homies and family members unleashed an ass whoopin' on the police that they will never forget. Bottles were thrown bustin' their dog asses in the face and all. People were coming to battle with everything they had not thinking for a second what the consequences would be. One of the officers had the upper hand against one of my folks and continuously struck him with his baton. Blood covered the young man's face as he lay on the ground trying to escape his attacker. Crawling in a backward motion and holding his arm in front of himself to shield his face was all he was able to do, ultimately resulting in his arm being broken in two places. When another one of our people caught a glimpse of the attack and went to assist I turned to follow suit. No sooner than I had attempted to do so the smell of the pepper spray released on another crowd of individuals sent me to coughing violently, bent over, holding my chest. The officer that attempted to stand toe-to-toe with me and pulled the ultimate bitch move just seconds ago hit me with his baton from behind causing me to stand up and try to grab my back. Before I could turn around he struck me again. Before long, even the onlookers joined in on the riot and the police department knew things were about to get ugly. They were completely outnumbered and had quickly become our victims instead of our authority figures. Squad cars had pulled up with police officers jumping out to be of assistance to the officers already on the scene and by the end of the whole incident six of us were in custody. Once again I was the only female amongst the crew who had gone to jail.

All of this had transpired over the way they treated Matt and his ass wasn't in jail, I was. He was at home doing whatever it was he wanted to do. The police were hot at me so using the phone was completely out of the question. I had to wait it out. After the booking process they placed me in a holding tank with two other bitches. One was a prostitute I later came to know as Sugar and the other was a dope fiend that I never got around to conversing with. Three cells over was a bunch of red rag bitches talking shit through the bars. None of it bothered me though. I was still in my own world thinking of how my brother was gone and I was sittin' in jail instead of wit' the family and friends at the repast if there was one. Things bitches let come out their mouth never bothered me too much anyway. It was the invasion of my body space that was a problem for me. Fuck what they be talkin' 'bout and how loud they felt the need to talk, give me three feet and we cool.

Once I snapped out of my little moment of disappointment, the rest of the time I spent in the concrete cell was kinda cool. My homies, who were locked up one the men's side just across the way, and I were crackin' jokes, fuckin' wit' the deputies, and talkin' about how crazy this whole little incident was. Might as well make the best of it, shit it was too late to be down and out, teary eyed, or stressed. The deputies were growing tired of our shit, especially the young lady that we had been clownin' for quite some time now because of her body odor.

"You know what I'm just about tired of your mouth," the deputy said as she approached my cell.

"And I'm just about tired of your smell masah," I said imitating a slave.

The whole cell block burst out in laughter causing her blood to boil. After witnessing the hostility of the red rag girls from the other cell she decided to pull a stunt of her own. "Let's see how tough you are now," she said while unlocking their cell to release two of the young ladies and unite them with me and the two other women in my cell. As soon as the gate closed one of the girls got crackin' wit' me.

"Fuck crabs!" she said loud, with authority, before hittin' me up with a cold two piece. Nothing came from my mouth after those words because no words were needed. We locked up in that cell like two pit bulls at a dog fight. Blows were thrown back and forth for a cool little minute until she kicked me in my stomach. Slumped over, holding my stomach, I tried my best to endure the pain. Soon as she lifted her leg to kick again I grabbed it and pulled her towards me, causing her to fall flat on her back. Now standing over her with a hand full of hair, I drug her about two feet to my right and commenced to bangin' her head against the steel bars.

"Blood you got me fucked up!" her friend yelled coming to her assistance.

BAM BAM BAM!

I felt the blows coming from behind, connecting with the back of my head at lightning speed. With my head down I attempted to swing and get myself out of this awkward position. When I finally did, I put my back up against the wall and got it in on her big ass. Shoulder to shoulder the bitch couldn't fade me but whenever she was able to grab me, it was all ova. Now this is where it really gets poppin'. My first attacker was now back in action runnin' up to do her thang but with my back against the wall I maintained my rank. Obviously tired of the ball in my court, the heavy set girl, also my second attacker grabbed my hair. With my head down, the two of them went in but I kept on swingin'. Now pulled down to the ground, I laid on my back kickin' and swingin' to prevent them from getting on top of me.

"Hold up! It ain't gone be none of this shit," the smoker lady said jumping in, aiding me in the fight. Her blows didn't really last too long but when she had nothing more left in her she jumped on the big girls back and started chokin' her ass out. While she handled that I came face to face with my first attacker and knocked her ass out. All of a sudden, the deputies swarm in to break everything up.

Once the girls were removed from my cell I leaned against the wall to catch my breath. Sugar, the prostitute girl, sat in the far corner looking at me. "What the fuck you lookin' at? If I wasn't tired I would beat *yo*' ass," I said to her while breathing hard.

The smoker lady came and stood by my side, "You cool?"

"Yeah I'm good. Good lookin' out," I said givin' her a handshake.

"Oh, don't trip. Just look out for me. Gimmie some of that good shit to smoke when we get out. I'mma give you my address okay." She spoke fast in a loud, firm tone.

I couldn't believe my ears but she was serious as hell. The whole cell block burst out in laughter again.

Two hours and twenty-five minutes later...

"Mr. Casmill! Damian Casmill! Let's go, you made bail," the short chubby deputy yelled as she walked to his cell inserting the key to release him.

"Aight Cuz! Movin!" Damian said while walking out the cell.

"Ke! Stay up baby and holla at ya boy!" he continued, talking to me while pointing in my direction and then holdin' his hand up to his face imitating a phone receiver.

"Aight big homie I'm right behind you. Movin' gang!"

That particular moment set my mind in motion. *Where was this nigga Matt at? I should have been the first bitch walkin' up outta here. He was my nigga and all, true enough. But if he let me sit up in here I got something for his ass.*

~$~

The next evening I made bail.

"Keshawn Flower! Let's go, you goin' home," Deputy Harris said like he was kind of disappointed. When I walked out of them double doors lookin' and smellin' like yesterday, Matt greeted me with a big hug and a statement that almost got him slapped.

"I know you enjoyed yo' night chillin' wit' the homies."

That shit was nowhere near funny but that silly ass laugh he gave would have made you think it was.

"Fuck you! You lucky you showed up, cause I was just beginning to plot on yo' ass. Now laugh at that!" I said smart mouthed in his face before kissing him.

"You thought you were plotting on me but what you were doin' was planning a homicide on the niggas you thought you were sendin'."

All I could do was smile and shake my head 'cause he wasn't lyin'. And that's why we loved each other, because we could speak our mind and we were one in the same. We were cool, calm, and collective but once we snapped it was over. We went all in with it whether by ourselves or together. Together though, we were a street sweepin' team, a real force to be reckoned with.

When we got home I went straight to the bathroom. My toothbrush became my best friend as I brushed my pearly whites and began running my bath water. The sound of warm running water was music to my ears and the sweet smell of my pear body wash I squeezed in the water made me dance to its tune. By the time I finished brushing my teeth the water level was just right. In a matter of seconds I was out of them clothes and in my birthday suit, climbing into the tub. I slid myself down under the water until the water covered my neck and closed my eyes. Relaxation at its finest, I thought to myself with the lavender and vanilla aromatherapy candles burning on the counter top and beside the bath tub. The water felt so good I nearly fell asleep. That is until my honey walked in. When he grabbed my washcloth and saturated it with my body wash I grew wide awake. He gently scrubbed my body from head to toe paying close attention to my most private places. When he washed between my legs my pussy immediately started to tingle. The softness of his lips added even more excitement to the equation causing me to moisten as he kissed me.

"Umm you-missed-me-huh?" I asked in between kisses. With his tongue dancing around in my mouth he nodded yes and began running water down my back with the squeeze of the towel. Once the soap was thoroughly rinsed from my body he lifted me from the tub which caused his muscles to flex and protrude through his shirt. I was wrapped in a towel, carried like a newlywed bride to the bedroom, and released from his muscular hold to lie on the bed. No sooner than my head had rested on its softness, my legs had been spread apart and placed over his shoulders. My thighs were caressed slowly but in sync with my clitoris. It was a warm, soft, pleasurable feeling that I had grown to appreciate and enjoy. With every stroke of his fingers my hips gyrated with them.

"Yes baby, oooooh do that shit," I whispered to him confirming he was definitely doin' his thang. As he inserted two fingers in my pussy I arched me back. The pleasure of both his fingers and the rapid stroking of his tongue against my clit sent my legs to shaking and my heart racing. My breathing had become very unsteady causing me to sound as if I were hyperventilating. Seeing that he had me right where he wanted me, Matt moved in for the kill. His tongue stopped its rapid motion and he began suckin' my clit like a newborn baby being breastfed. His fingers went in as deep as they could and back out again, while one finger from the other hand was used to penetrate my ass. My butt cheeks clinched together and I fought to move his hand but to no avail. My legs squeezed tightly around his neck caused him to remove his finger and try spreading my legs just as he did I found ecstasy.

"AWWW! Oh shiiiitttt!!" I screamed loud enough for the neighbors to hear while my body went into convulsions.

I climaxed like never before leaving his face lookin' like a glazed donut. Unable to move due to the weakness of my legs, I laid there for a while, while I recovered from my much needed sex attraction. After regaining my composure and the strength in my legs I went back in the bathroom to take a quick shower.

"Damn I love you!" was all I said when I entered the bathroom kissing him on his neck and preparing for my shower.

"Hahaha yeah right!" Matt laughed. "You love that head I be givin' yo' ass."

Peeping out the shower from behind the shower curtain I said, "you muthafuckin' right!" and laughed back at him while dousing him with a cup full of ice cold water that I grabbed off of the nightstand before entering the bathroom.

"What the fuck was that for?"

"Nigga don't try that shit again. Next time you do I'm gonna slide something in yo' ass!"

"Yeah okay."

Matt and I were past all that I love you shit. Neither one of us were wit' the whole I love you game. We accepted the fact that we both knew the business and each other's true feelings so why keep repeating it every day. I know that sounds crazy but shit it is what it is. To be honest I think that was just my way of protecting my feelings from being one day destroyed by his actions. Later that day he decided he wanted to take me out. On the way there we seen four enemy niggas hangin' on the corner and we flipped into Bonnie and Clyde mode. He jumped out on them niggas and commenced to whoopin' their asses. Two of them tore ass down the street and I jumped behind the wheel of the truck and proceeded to run their asses down. While one got away with nothing but a graze to the side the second victim suffered severe bodily damage from being hit by the truck which sent him flying in the air like superman before landing on the windshield like a meteor falling from the sky. Maybe it was just the adrenaline or possibly the thought of losing his life but he jumped up running once again. This time it was with a limp. The .380 I had in the stash was now cocked and ready to go as I jumped out in pursuit of my victim.

BOOM!

He hit the ground wit with one hand and on one knee in a runner stance.

BOOM!

He fell forward completely on his stomach as I walked swiftly in his direction arm stretched out gripping my weapon and reaching his presence. My footsteps alarmed him that his maker was near. With all his strength he managed to turn over. When his eyes met mines, fear took over his body and for all the right reasons.

"Please…"

BOOM! BOOM! BOOM!

"Game over!"

Gunshots rang out from around the corner where I had just left Matt. Without hesitation I ran back to the truck and smashed in his direction. When I reached the corner of which he was last seen a body laid lifelessly on the ground faced down in a growing puddle of blood. I looked around in search of Matt and noticed someone running down the street.

"Please let this be him," I said to myself in route to pick him up, and it was.

"Baby, hop in!"

He jumped in and we took off with no words exchanged and headed to a room.

Chapter Three

A shower and two hours later we arrived back at home. Matt's phone was blowin' up from people having a million questions and a lot of concern. No one knew who the perpetrators were but since it happened just a few blocks within our home, verifying that he wasn't one of the male victims they talked about on TV during a breaking news broadcast, was of top priority. Happy with their findings the phone calls stopped and we changed clothes and headed out to dinner.

The Spaghetti Factory in Hollywood was the shit. They had the best pasta ever. Walking into the restaurant was like walking into an old movie. Hand painted murals covered the walls and booths resembling old train coaches were spread throughout. A young Caucasian girl approached us with big crystal blue eyes, blonde hair pulled back into a ponytail, her old fashioned uniform on and menus in her hand.

"Welcome to the Spaghetti Factory. Right this way please," and led us to one of the booths that sat in the center of the dining room. Once seated, we ordered our food and decided on soda for our drinks. There was no need for the wait because we both knew what we wanted.

"So that'll be one lasagna extra garlic bread with a Cesar salad, one order of spaghetti with Italian sausage, a garden salad, and two Sprites. Will that be all for you?"

"Yeah that's it."

"Okay. I'll be right back with your drinks."

As she sashayed off to put in our order Matt's eyes were low key glued to her ass but I don't miss a beat. Without causing a scene I put one foot between his legs underneath the table and slid down in my seat to apply pressure. His eyes grew bigger from the sudden pressure before sayin', "what the-" and as calmly as I possibly could, I winked at him sayin', "For every action there's a reaction. Don't forget what kinda bitch you got sittin' here at this table."

"You got me fucked up. Don't start no shit up in here KeKe." He tried his hardest to stand his ground but we both knew the statement I just made was real; no games, no sarcasm, just real live shit.

When the waitress returned with our drink order I looked to Matt for any sign of rebellion towards what I had just said and there was none. He respected my take on the situation and was sure to direct his undivided attention where it should have been this whole time. Right here at this table. Dinner turned out to be a very wonderful thing. The food was delicious; we shared a few laughs, and talked about all types of things. We even laughed about the incident that just occurred moments ago. With the bill paid and tip on the table I decided to make my way to the restroom while Matt went to get our vehicle. No sooner than I had gotten away from Matt I found myself caught off guard and tryin' to catch my balance.

BRIDGE 2 DESTRUCTION

"Aw damn! What up lil mama," a strange, unfamiliar dude said after bumpin' into me hard enough to cause my body to jerk back almost losing my balance. It took everything in me to hold my tongue. A look of disgust was all he got in return as I observed him from head to toe. Tall, brown skinned, hazel green eyes, curly brown hair and a gold tooth in the front of his mouth. His clothes were baggie but fit him just right and he wore big flashy jewelry. I had no idea who he was or why the fuck he was sayin' what up instead of excuse me or my bad after bumpin' into me, but what I did know was his face was locked into my memory bank. If I'd ever run into him again it wouldn't be friendly. I wanted to go crazy on him and attempt to knock his head off but Hollywood was the wrong place to do street business considering this was police headquarters. They patrolled the streets of Hollywood so much and so thick that you'd think the fuckin' president spent every part of his day and night out here.

I wondered to myself, "Would this nigga have tried me had he seen me walking with Matt? Better yet, would he have had the same take on the situation if he had bumped into Matt instead of me?" As much as I wanted to tell Matt about what had just happened I didn't. Bringing up the subject to him would have caused big problems so instead of doing so, when he pulled the car around to where I was I just let it be. But I swear that nigga did that shit on purpose and couldn't anybody tell me different.

"Baby don't forget we gotta go pick up Mai," I slammed the door shut and buckled my seatbelt. School is back in session tomorrow so all of her fun is over.

"You wanna go pick her up now?"

"Shit that's up to you. Are we done hangin' out for the night?"

"Yeah we could call it a night. I miss my little princess anyway."

Matt loved Mai like she was his own. Since he had a great sense of humor and was a kid at heart Mai couldn't help but love him too. He gave her his undivided attention and played every game you could possibly think of with her. He even helped with homework and took her on play dates.

TG went to jail shortly after being released from the hospital and was sentenced to fifteen years in prison. As we drove down the 110 freeway I thought of how fucked up it was for Mai to end up in this situation but at the same time was grateful for the role Matt had took on in her life to fill that void. Though she was too young to really remember him, as time went on I faithfully reminded her of who her father was. Pictures, phone calls, and anything else I could think of giving her I made sure I did it. I just wanted her to know him, love him and respect him. He did some foul shit but he was a good father and he loved Mai to death. That's one thing I would never take from him especially since I wasn't one of those miserable ass bitches holdin' their kids over their baby daddy's heads. Regardless of whether we were together or not, he was her father and it wasn't my job to come in between that.

Snapping back into reality I realized we were already here. "I was wonderin' when you were gonna get out," Matt said.

"Forget you. I was thinkin' about somethin'."

After releasing my seatbelt from its buckle I climbed out of the car and headed for the door. Halfway down the walkway the door of the house flung open and Mai came running out with her purse dangling from her shoulder.

"Mommie!"

I braced myself for her signature move as she jumped into my arms and gave me a big hug.

"Hey princess! What are you doing up and full of all this energy?"

Laughing from my fingers tickling her up under her arm, she squirmed and said, "Auntie made me take a nap and I woke up when it was dark already."

"She did? Well let me talk to Auntie and you go get in the car wit Matt."

Why did I say that? When her feet touched the ground she took off down the walkway like Speedy Gonzalez. Ready for her usual act of love, the car door was opened & Matt had his hands stretched out to pick her up. She climbed right on top of him hugging him and sharing the contents of her purse. Matt pretended to be very interested in the things she showed him and Mai loved every minute of it.

"Thanks sis! I appreciate you watching her for me. I'll holla at you tomorrow."

"No problem. Call me when ya'll make it home."

~$~

While I prepared things for the next morning my M&M's (Matt and Mai) were playing their hearts out on the play station we had in the living room sitting on the very bottom of the entertainment center. The fifty-inch TV screen made the players look life-sized to Mai. For hours they engaged in an all-out war on the video game. All of their arguing, laughing, and giggling made me tired. Shit, I gave Mai a bath and before I knew it I was in bed and sound asleep. What time they went to bed I had no idea.

Chapter Four

"Rock the boat / Rock the boat / change positions…" Aaliyah blasted from the speakers scaring the shit out of me. Either it was just me or someone had turned up the volume on the radio causing the alarm to be more of a disturbance than a wake-up call. I turned the alarm off and made my way to the bedroom down the hall to wake up Mai.

"Rise and shine mommies princess," I sung as I turned on the light but Mai wasn't in the bed. The linen was still intact like no one had ever even slept there. Now that I think about it, Matt wasn't in bed when I got up either. "I know they better not be in here playin' this damn game," I said to myself as I entered the living room only to find that empty too. "What the fuck?" Starting to panic, I dialed Matt's number and got no answer. When I dialed it again I noticed the phone vibrating on the dresser. Now I was really nervous. Where could they possibly be, and without his phone? He never left his phone. The police could run up in here right now and before he makes an escape out this house that phone would be scooped up and taken with him. The kitchen, I thought to myself and when I dashed around the corner out of the hallway they were sitting at the table eating cereal smiling at me.

"Y'all scared the shit outta me!"

My M&M's laughed and gave each other a high five. "I told you if we were quiet she wouldn't find us," Matt whispered to Mai.

"I'll deal wit' you when I get her off to school," I said pointing at Matt as I took my seat at the table in front of a bowl marked, Mommie, written in purple crayon. While eating my cereal, the small television we had sitting on the kitchen counter displayed an update on the South Los Angeles Shooting. "Turn it up babe.

Turn it up!" I said jumping up and down, pointing at the TV with milk just about ready to drip from my mouth. Matt rushed over and did as I asked.

"Today authorities are asking for the public's help in identifying the second shooter. The only description authorities have gathered on one of the suspects is African American with a small build wearing a black hoodie. If anyone knows anything that can possibly help bring this person to justice you are urged to call the 77th Street Police Department. A memorial will be held tonight in memory of eight-year-old Bianca Taylor at six p.m. and the community is expected to attend in very high numbers. Reporting live from…" Matt turned down the TV and ordered Mai to go cleanup for school.

While she washed her hands and face, Matt and I talked about the seriousness of the news broadcast. "I really hope Kai didn't see that," I said shaking my head, worried that my sister would slip back into depressed mode. Then my phone started ringin'.

"She seen it," Matt said sarcastically. And true enough when I picked up my phone the caller id displayed Kai's number. Before I could say hello, Kai started talkin'. She went on and on about what she should do and as soon as I could get a word in I said, "Kai I can't talk to you on this phone. I'll be there in a minute."

"Fuck. What was I thinkin' about? You're right, my bad. I'll see you when you get here. This shit just really got me fucked up."

"I know, but calm down. I'll see you in a minute."

Matt had already dressed Mai and her hair was braided so after I brushed my teeth and shit we left the house. As we approached the front of the school, kids were running and playing as they entered the school grounds. When my car came to a complete stop Mai followed suit. My eyes were glued to her as she pranced her way into school, ponytails flopping up and down resembling that of Pippy Longstocking. I don't know what I would do if something happened to my baby. I love her more than anything in this world. One day I'm gonna shake this hood shit and give her a better life, I promised myself. All throughout the day as I handled my business I thought about changing for the better. If not for me, at least for my daughter. She deserved more than what I had when I was coming up and she was gonna get all that she deserved.

HONK!

A loud horn broke me from my trance while sitting at a green light. The driver that just seconds ago sat behind me went around givin' me the middle finger while flying past me almost hitting another car in the process. Two blocks ahead of me was an emerald green Lexus that I was sure to be Matt's. As I pulled up alongside of him, through the passenger side mirror, I noticed a gun stretched out of the window of the car behind him. The unidentified man let loose before I could say a word shattering the rear window of the Lexus. Trying to shelter myself from the rapid gun fire I laid down in the seat of my car and bust open the stash to retrieve my gun. Looking over to Matt's car I noticed he was hit but the unidentified man was now trying to getaway. My first instinct was to make sure my nigga was okay but if I let this bitch ass nigga get away I would never forgive myself. With that thought in mind my speedometer went from zero to ninety in record breaking time. The silver Impala had raced through a yellow light at the intersection of Century and Broadway with me right on his tail. We looked like we were fresh out of the movie Fast and Furious. He must have thought I was just trying to make the light because when we approached the red signal light on 108th he stopped. What killed me was the unexpected sight of a man I wasn't quite ready to see. Pulling alongside of him with my passenger window at its halfway point, he turned and looked at me with that same devious smile from before.

"Aw shit, what's up lil mama" replayed in my mind like a broken record. *This muthafucka!* I thought to myself. I knew the day he bumped into me at the Spaghetti Factory that he had purposely done so. What I didn't know was I would run into him again this soon. When my window disappeared into the door panel that sparkling glare from my .380 flipped his smile upside down. With that same devious smile he gave me and a wink of the eye I said, "What up lil daddy?!" and emptied my clip on his bitch ass leavin' him slumped over his steering wheel.

~$~

Back at the scene in which Matt got hit the police had already swarmed the area. Yellow tape stretched out along the parameter of the crime scene. The ambulance was just pulling off as I came walking around the block. One of the bystanders leaving the scene walked in my direction shaking her head in disbelief.

"What happened over there?" I asked her to find out what she knew.

"Somebody got shot and another person was nearly killed. These streets just keep getting worse and worse."

Wait... another person? What the hell was she talking about?

"Oh it was two people in the car?" I asked to clarify her last statement.

"Yeah his girlfriend was in the passenger seat. Poor child might not make it."

My heart hit my feet, my adrenaline began rushing, and tears flowed from my eyes. This bitch gotta be mistaking. I didn't see anybody in the car when I pulled up, or did I? My mind was racing one hundred miles per hour trying to relive that crazy moment but no matter how hard I tried I couldn't remember anything but that gun in my side view mirror. Overwhelmed with mixed emotions and no longer able to hold my composure I made way to my car and drove to the hospital. Killa King a.k.a. Martin Luther King Jr. Hospital, is where he or, they, were transported. When I got to the hospital the only thing on my mind was getting inside to see him and get to the bottom of things. With my mind racing and in detective mode I parked the car and ran to the emergency entrance, never noticing I had parked in the handicapped zone. Once I checked in at the ER window, the admitting clerk advised me to have a seat while the doctors did their job. Looking around for a seat was harder than finding a parking spot. Patients of all types flooded the waiting room along with friends and family members providing love and support through whatever sickness or injuries they had endured. A patient's name was called over the intercom leaving four seats available. Swiftly moving toward the seat before someone else could take them, I found myself occupying a seat next to a man with a broken arm and bleeding through the towel he held firmly against his head. I sat in that chair contemplating what it was I wanted to say. What questions would I ask? And for hours I felt a sense of betrayal that I never thought I'd feel. While battling with these emotions familiar faces began to flood through the ER doors asking to see him. I sat in silence waiting and wanting someone to disclose *her* name, but no one ever did.

"What's up KeKe? How's he doin'?" Big Choc asked me while occupying the seat next to me. All I could do was shrug my shoulders because I had no idea. I was waiting just as well as them.

"What did you hear happened?" I asked her hoping to get the missing information I was looking for.

Looking as if she didn't want to answer the question she said, "Shit I don't know, only that the homie was shot."

Smiling that devious smile I shook my head and replied, "Okay! Yeah okay, I'm out of here."

Before I could grab my things Choc asked, "Damn, what's wrong wit you?"

"Nothin' Choc, don't trip. I'm outta here though. Y'all do this shit 'cause I'm not." When I got in my car I noticed my phone was lit up. There were seventeen missed calls and fourteen of 'em was Kai. My mind wasn't in the right place to talk to her at the moment so I cleared the calls and made a mental note to call her as soon as I calmed down.

The drive home had me feelin' real fucked up. I did it all wit this nigga and gave him wholehearted love. Now here I was, confused, outraged about the whole ordeal. I was an emotional train wreck wondering was he okay? Was all this time and effort I put into him for nothing? Was he cheating on me? Did he love me? Too many questions, no answers, and not enough courage to face them even if there had been. Hot as Cheyenne pepper and no way to vent, tears flooded my eyes and continued to do so until I fell asleep. About twelve o'clock that night my phone rang loudly on the nightstand. I opened my eyes looking in its direction then after two more rings I finally answered.

"Talk."

"Bitch where the fuck you been? I been callin' you all fuckin' day and you ain't answered the phone, called back or nothing." Kai was angry as hell.

"My bad sis. I was on my way to yo' house when I saw Matt in traffic and some nigga pulled up and shot his car up. Shit got ugly from there and I was too turnt up to call you. I planned on callin' you soon as I calmed down but I fell asleep. You straight though?"

"Hell naw. I'm over here losin' my mind. Don't trip though we can just talk about it tomorrow. Is Matt okay?"

"Girl I don't know but the way I'm feelin' right about now, he's better off laid up in that hospital."

Kai laughed. "Girl, leave my brother-in-law alone."

"Fuck you and yo' brother-in-law," I said back. "I'll call you in the a.m. okay sis. I love you."

"Me too."

The phone was hung up and I attempted to fall back to sleep. About thirty minutes later the phone rings again causing me to become frustrated and angry.

"What?"

"What?! Is that anyway to greet yo' man?"

I wanted to smile at the sound of his voice but my heart wouldn't let me. "What you want Matt?" I dragged from being exhausted and irritated.

"Can you come see me in the morning, damn? Why you actin' like that?"

"Who was in the car wit' you?"

"What?"

"Either you gone answer me or I'm hangin' up. You heard what the fuck I said!"

True enough I loved this man to death but at the same time I was in no mood to play his game.

"Okay KeKe, look. It was Kandi. But wait! It ain't what you think. I was just giving her a ride."

"Okay," I said in an attempt to stay calm. "I'm not feeling well so I'll see you in the a.m."

"Alright. I love you."

The dial tone greeted his ear with those last words. *He love me,* ha. That's funny- a dead giveaway that somethin' wasn't right. We didn't do the whole I luv you thing now here he was sayin' it as if that was supposed to redirect my attention off of the situation at hand. Flipping out would have been too much like right so I played my position and pretended to be okay.

To add even more fuel to the fire, another female surfaced at the hospital during visiting hours the next morning. She obviously didn't know who I was 'cause she called him Daddy. It was like a dagger to the heart being twisted, pushed and pulled all at the same time. Matt knew the direction things were about to go in. His face told it all. If he had the ability to get out of that bed ole girl would have gotten the shit slapped outta her, but since he couldn't, the only thing he did was look shocked and put his head down shaking' it in disappointment. As calmly as I possibly could I grabbed my purse and said, "You know what? I'll just go."

Matt grabbed my arm in mid stride as I tried walking out the door. It was like a rehearsed movie. He put a firm hold on my arm resulting in me looking at my arm then looking to him. My face said *let me go*, while my mouth asked, "Are you sure you want this?" His eyes met mines and said *yes,* while his visitor attempted to say *no* and caught a quick left hook to the jaw. "Bitch I will..." Her weak ass falling against a medical cart was a clear invitation to come fuck wit' me but she decided against it and grabbed her things.

"Bitch! –," she began saying while walking out the door.

Not the least bit worried about her or her threats, I held my arms out at both sides welcoming her to come embrace this ass whooping I had waiting on her. Just as I assumed, she didn't want it with me. Since she kept walking I directed my attention and frustration toward Matt and began punching on his ass like he was a human punching bag. Nurses stormed into the room trying to defuse the situation but caused an even bigger problem. Putting your hands on me when I was angry was the wrong thing to do. It made me feel like a child being chastised by her parents and I wasn't havin' it. The first nurse to touch me got fired on, just like the bitch that just left and I dared anyone else to touch me. It was plenty more where that came from. Numerous threats were made in getting me arrested but it didn't matter. The way I feel right now; fuck them, fuck this hospital and fuck how they feel. None of them knew my name and Matt definitely wasn't gon' tell 'em. I wished the fuck he would. Before security or police could get to his room I was almost at my car headed back home.

I knew I should have just went to Kai's house, I thought to myself. As a matter of fact, that's exactly what I'm about to do. The next light I busted a right and jumped on the freeway headed west, to Kai's house. When I got there she was in the garage washing clothes. When I parked my car she put her hands on her hips and looked at me like I was crazy or somethin'.

"Don't look at me like that."

"Girl, I'm glad I wasn't ova here dyin' cause you sho' wasn't gon' come and rescue me. I would have been dead."

"I know. I know. Don't go hard on me though 'cause I got enough goin' on. So what's up? Tell me what's goin on with you."

"I don't know what to do KeKe. I can't deal wit this shit man. If they are lookin for the second shooter then I got a problem. That means Bianca was shot with more than one gun and we both know it wasn't yours."

"Stop jumpin' to conclusions. They probably just wanna see what they can find out because they know somebody else was there. Shit, somebody had to shoot ole boy. He didn't shoot himself. Plus, I was the one wearing a black hoodie not you."

"I never looked at it like that. I can do some jail time but not for no little kid. They gon' hang my ass from the top of them bars in there for some shit like that."

"Shut the fuck up. You ain't goin' to jail."

"What if somebody seen us?"

"Ain't nobody seen us except for that punk ass Keontay dude. And I doubt if he says anything 'cause he know like we know, we got them boys in there that'll put his ass to sleep-sleep."

"On da real. See if yo' ass would have come yesterday and said this shit, I wouldn't have been so stressed out for the whole goddamn day."

"Come on my nigga. I said my bad, damn! Quick question though before I get up outta here."

"What's up?"

"You know the funeral is tomorrow at one. Are you gon' go?"

"Naw. I don't think I'm ready for that. That's kinda risky too don't you think?"

"Shit, maybe. That's why I plan on bein' in the background wit' mines. I just won't feel right if I don't go."

"Well, be careful bitch," she said huggin' me like an oversized teddy bear. "All da time, baby."

Chapter Five

Just in case / I don't make it home tonight / let me make love....,

Damn I know it's not time to get up already, I thought hitting the snooze button on the alarm clock radio. Climbing out of bed with squinting eyes, dragging my feet, and yawning loudly, I made it down the hall to enter Mai's room, waking her up as I turned on the lights. "Time to get up princess," I said while yawning.

After spending most of the night tossing and turning with frustration, my mind and body wasn't on the same accord. My mind was pumped and determined to stick to the routine, starting with getting Mai off to school. But my body was exhausted saying, Fuck that, go back to sleep. The battle between my mind and body continued on as a draw until breakfast and a hot shower rejuvenated me leaving my mind victorious again.

"Mommy, why Matt wasn't home?"

"He left early for work," I told her hoping to end the conversation before it went any further.

"Then, why he didn't kiss me like he always do?"

"He did. You were just too tired to feel it."

"Then why he didn't...,"

"MAI!" With my hand over my face massaging my temples, I calmly and softly said, "Baby please stop askin' me a million questions. Mommy has a headache but we'll talk about it later, okay."

Sad and disappointed by my reaction to her questions she mumbled, "Okay," and looked to the floor shamefully.

Snapping on my baby was wrong. I never yell at her and now that I have I feel real fucked up. This whole ordeal wit Matt has me on and I really need to shake this shit off. Pulling up to Mai's school I leaned over and gave her a kiss, Umm-mwah! "Sorry for yelling at you baby. I didn't mean to yell at you and I promise I won't ever do it again, okay?"

"Okay, Mommy."

"I love you."

"I love you too."

"Now get on in there and show them who's gonna be running thangs one day," I said tapping her on the leg as she got ready to exit the car. As she disappeared into the crowd my phone rang.

"What up?"

"Are you comin' to visit me today? Or, are you still turnt up?"

"Matt, I ain't comin' back up there."

"Why not?"

BRIDGE 2 DESTRUCTION

"Number one, I'm not in the mood for no more surprises. Two, I really ain't 'bout to go back to jail, and three, I got better thangs to do."

"Better thangs to do? Cuz, you serious?"

"Hell yeah I'm serious. Nigga you done fucked wit' the wrong one, and don't call me Cuz."

"Cuz, don't get at me like that. I don't fuck wit' none of these bitches in the streets. They want me to but I don't."

"Whatever Matt. You heard me, I didn't stutter. I'll see you when you get home. Tell yo' bitches to come see you."

"Ke...!" the dial tone took in the remainder of his sentence 'cause I didn't wanna hear it. I love this man but I'll be damned if I let him send me through all this shit. I gotta figure out a way to hold this shit together, and at the same time teach him a lesson. TG played me the same way so now everything is about me and my baby.

~$~

Since I had a few hours before Bianca's funeral, I decided to go ahead and do some cleaning and a little shopping. The radio was turned up on full blast and the oil burner was burnin' sending off a sweet aroma called Sweet Dreams. It was a soft, fruity smell that made your visitors wanna stay around a while. The living room took all of thirty minutes to clean. All it needed was a little dusting and for the games and cd's to be put away. Mai had a few toys layin' around but nothin' outrageous.

By the time I had gotten to the bedroom I was in complete groove mode. While making the bed I sung and swayed all over the room enjoying this time to myself. When I picked up Matts belongings off of the floor I began to get agitated. I'm tired of cleanin' up behind his grown ass. How hard is it to pick up your clothes and put 'em in the hamper? After doin' that I picked up his hoodie to hang it in the closet and all of his contents fell out on the floor. "Shhhhh," I sighed as I bent down to pick everything up. On the back of a business card was lip prints that some girl wearing pink lipstick must have put on there followed by a message that read, "Call me when you want some more of this," with the phone number underneath. My blood started to boil as I continued picking everything up and threw it in his drawer. The dresser drawer slammed close causing the dresser to shake. The longer I stood there the more I wished it was his ass I used all of my strength on and not that dresser. It took everything in me to let it go and continue on with what I was doin', but I did. When I finished the bedroom, of course the kitchen and the bathroom came next. Mai's room was cool and the little things she did have outta place, she could take care of on her own when she got home.

With the house clean and smelling good I ran me a hot bubble bath so I could relax. While the water ran I searched the closet for somethin' nice to wear to the funeral. After rumbling through the closet for a while, picking through the ridiculously large amount of clothes I had, I decided on a navy blue business suit with some silver heels. Once my clothes were laid across the bed, it was time to turn off the water. Sliding out of my clothes I looked in the mirror admiring my body then stepped into the tub and slid down into the water. The water along with the steam that filled the room gave me a sense of relief. For the moment, I was relaxed, calm, and totally in another world. Had it not been for this funeral I'd stay in here all day. After soaking for about twenty minutes I decided to wash up and get started with my day.

The radio was still bumpin' causing me to sway side to side, singin' it's tune, while getting dressed. Standing in the mirror, the end result of my little make over session was pleasing. My hair was teased hanging loosely over my right shoulder, my lips were poppin' and the Gucci shades sealed the deal. *Damn I'm fly*, I thought to myself. I know all bitches wish they can pull it together this good without a fashion designer and all that ridiculous ass make-up and shit.

As I walked out the door I blew out the candle burning on the oil burner, turned off the radio, and opened the blinds. "Okay KeKe," I said to myself, "let's do this." Not wanting to stand out too much at the funeral I decided to drive my little low key Nissan Maxima. Before heading to the church I decided to stop by my homeboy's Hip Hop Clothing Store and see what hot new arrivals they had. Nothin' really caught my eye except for this Louise Vuitton purse that belonged to one of the customers. "Y'all ain't got shit in here today dang," I said to the sells representative before walkin' out the door. *Let me get my ass to this church. I don't have no business shoppin' anyway*, I thought to myself.

When I pulled up to the church everyone was there; teachers, kids, family, friends, people from the neighborhood and the police. I didn't get out of the car because I wasn't sure if that was a smart idea. But I sat behind the tent on my windows looking at all that went on. From where I was sitting I could see that Freda and Charmaine did a good job on the ceremony. The family wore different shades of yellow along with black. They all looked so beautiful. Charmaine must have spent the entire week getting' sober and cleaning herself up because for a while I didn't even notice who she was. Yellow flowers of different shades were spread throughout and leading through the entrance of the church. People wore white ribbons that marked the date of Bianca's death along with a sunflower with her picture in the middle of it. As bad as I wanted to go in, I knew it would be a mistake.

After about an hour and a half of sitting in the car people began to exit the church full of tears. Anger was displayed all over their faces from the thought of this innocent child being slain so young. Shortly thereafter, the pallbearers made their exit carrying the smallest casket I'd ever seen at a funeral. It was pearl white with gold trimming and sparkled in the glare of the sun. When everyone made it to their cars I pulled out and headed toward the cemetery. There was no sense in me waiting on them, especially since there was no need for them to see me anyway. Freda and Charmaine knew I would be in attendance and that was all that mattered to me.

Forest Lawn was a bit of a drive but I made it there in good timing. When I entered the gate I stopped at the large booth that occupied the center of the cemeteries' entrance and asked the information clerk for the directions to the burial site for Bianca Taylor. With the directions in my hand, I drove up the pathway leading to the top of the hill where the clerk said Bianca's final resting place would be located and waited for the family to come in. From the top of the hill you could see a spectacular view of the city and it was peaceful. While up there I thought of all the time I've known Bianca and all the moments we shared together. She was always so happy, so excited, and well mannered. I gave her anything she wanted because I see so much of me in her. She was a reflection of me and I

BRIDGE 2 DESTRUCTION

wanted so badly to see all the good in me, erasing the bad as if it never happened. And now that image of me that I wanted to hold on to so badly, along with the person who truly carried that image was gone, I was badly broken.

Tears built up in my eyes, followed by an overwhelming amount of anger, and I found myself flippin' out, cryin' profusely. All of these feelings I carried deep inside my soul and today, at this moment, it was time to let it out. I was going crazy up on this hill and on nobody but the wind. By the time I pulled myself together a long line of cars came driving in my direction. Just like at the church, my plan was to sit in the car but my heart wouldn't let me. Instead I stood at a distance watching as they released doves in the air. They flew around and around for quite some time before flying to the point where they had become a little white dot in the sky.

I was so caught up in the burial and focusing on the doves in the sky that I hadn't noticed the large numbers of police that quietly surrounded me. With guns drawn from every direction officers yelled, "Put your hands in the air!" I looked around in disbelief and stood there completely noncompliant with what they said. "Put your hands in the air," they repeated one more time, this time cocking their guns preparing for the worse. Charmaine could be seen running in my direction with a look of fear on her face. Through all the yelling and screaming the cops were doin' I heard Charmaine say, "Please do what they say." Immediately after, I put my hands in the air. Still standing at a distance the police ordered me to put my hands on my head, drop to my knees, lay faced down on the ground, and stretch out my arms. I followed their rules as they were called out but everything in me wanted to run from the time I noticed them. If I had, I would have been dead right along with Bianca. Police hurried over, guns still drawn and manhandled me up off the ground. While leading the way to the car they read me my rights and asked me my full name. I didn't respond. I had nothing to say. My mind was racing one hundred miles per hour with thoughts of my own child. Her father has been gone almost her whole entire life, Matt was laid up in the hospital, and now here I was slammed face first into the back of a police car. Again!

~$~

BRIDGE 2 DESTRUCTION

At the station it seemed as if every officer in the building was awaiting my arrival. The moment we walked in all eyes were on me. Some nodded with approval, some clapped, while others looked angry. "Take her to interview room B," one of the officers instructed. Doing just that, the officer that held a tight grip on my arm, guided me into the interrogation room and released my hands from behind my back. After sitting in the wooden chair my right arm was handcuffed to a metal bar attached to the wall, linking through the chairs back. "Someone will be in in a few," the officer said while exiting the room.

Ten minutes later, two officers entered the room introducing themselves. "Hello Ms. Flower. My name is Detective Banks and this is my partner, Detective Zamora. First of all would you like anything to drink; a soda, coffee, or water?" I sat silently shaking my head. "No. Okay. Well let me start by asking you, do you know why you're here today?" Still I sat silently in the chair giving the officer complete eye contact. "Did you hear me," he asked unsure of my ability to hear what he was saying. "Okay well maybe you wouldn't mine telling us where you were last Saturday afternoon." Again he got nothin'. He quickly became irritated and slammed his fist down on the table. "Damn it! I'm not about to play games with you. Look at this little girl, look at her," he yelled while spreading photos of Bianca's lifeless body all over the table. "She was eight-years-old for Christ sake. Now she's dead! What type of a monster are you? What were you thinkin'?" I looked at the officer with that same blank stare from before and still said nothing. He got so upset that he grabbed me up from the chair by my shirt then slammed me back down with one of his fist balled up as if he wanted to knock my head off. As his partner grabbed him off of me I smiled a devious smile and shook my head at him. All that was left for them to do is exit the room until they calmed down.

How did I know this was the reason they picked me up, I asked myself. This bitch ass nigga must be runnin' his mouth. Bet I get somebody to reach out and touch his ass, I thought to myself. It took the officers about twenty minutes to re-enter the room. Just as I expected they came in playin' the baby card. "You obviously didn't care about your victim being a child so we've decided we'll take your child from you and see how you like that." The officer was sure he would break me with that but he was mistaken. "Hey check this out. I'm not fo' all ya'lls bullshit so if you takin' me to jail take me. If not, leave me the fuck alone so I can go," I said as serious as a heart attack. For hours on in after that they asked me question after question and accused me of everything they could but just like the beginning of this interrogation, I had nothing to say. We stared at each other at a virtual stale mate. It was so thick in the room it would have been difficult for a chainsaw to cut through it. The stale mate went on for quite some time before I surrendered. My eyes wandered around the room taking in the awful sight of the room. The walls were filthy like no one has cleaned them since the jail has been in existence. Gang members from previous visits to this place had carved their hoods in the table as well as the chair I occupied at the moment. Simple act of marking their territory. The smell was stale and stuffy desperately in need of some air circulation. I can't do this, I thought to myself. Then the wooden door ajared revealing yet another deputy.

"Stand to your feet for me please," he said grabbing his keys to unlock the cuffs. For a moment I was sure I was goin' home. Then the harsh reality hit when the deputy replied, "You're under arrest".

Before I knew it I was bein' transported to the women's facility by homicide detectives to start the booking process.

~$~

"We got forty-eight hours to build a case against her or else we're going to have to release her."

"Don't be so sure about that," Deputy Zamora said walking past the interview room waving a piece of paper in the air. "I have here a statement from Mr. Keontay Bridges that puts Ms. Flower at the scene of the crime. I believe this is enough for a search warrant fellas."

The officers high-fived each other and made the necessary call to get the warrant they needed to find that one piece of evidence that they thought would ultimately prove their case. While Deputy Zamora made the call, Detective Banks rallied up the gang task force to begin discussing their tactics to serving the in-home search warrant.

"Alright boys, today we are going to search the home of Keshawn Flower. She's suspected of murdering Bianca Taylor. It's important that we do this by the book. We're looking for anything that can tie her to the crime; guns, ammunition, anything of that sort. Her last known address is also the address of one of her partners in crime who's also known to be armed and dangerous. Enter with caution, stay alert, and let's all make it home safe."

By the closing of his speech Deputy Zamora surfaced with the warrant. As soon as he did the team of officers assigned to this case wasted no time mounting up and heading to their destination. At least four cars, each containing four officers, pulled up to the house. When Detective Banks gave the signal to move, they emerged from the cars, surrounding the house in preparation to make their entrance. With everybody in position he gave the order for officer to move in.

The door came crashing in with so much force that the wood crumbled around the edges and came of the hinges. "Police! We have a search warrant," the officers yelled as they swarm the house with guns drawn ready to take out the first person who made a wrong move. Room after room they found no one. Once the house was declared clear Officer Zamora radioed Detective Banks, "all clear". With that said, they began their search, destroying the house and all of its contents.

After a long, frustrating, and unproductive search Detective Banks is relieved to hear an officer down the hall announcing he got something. Banks entered the room to find his colleague in possession of an aluminum box containing a long-nosed .22 caliber hand gun. The box was lined with a thick suede material holding the gun in perfect place. Even Banks had to admit the gun was a beauty. The handle was ivory trimmed in gold and the chrome was polished to perfection causing a mesmerizing sparkle to generate from it. A smile spread across his face and the gun was placed in a plastic zip-lock bag marked evidence. Nothing else was found in the house so the team prepared to make their exit. A copy of the warrant was left on the table along with Detective Banks business card.

The house was a disaster. Mattresses were flipped upside down, clothes and shoes were thrown from the closets, drawers were pulled out and tossed on the floor, and cabinets were opened and stripped of anything that they felt needed to be removed. When Shawna gets home, she is gonna be beyond pissed.

Chapter Six

Damn I can't believe I'm sittin in here. Looking out this window got me turnt up. The more I watched people walking through the city's streets the more I realized I had messed up. Pedestrians walked past the facility continuously, laughing, talking, and even listening to music through their headphones. All of them had a destination in mind; they all had somewhere to be or someone to see. I, on the other hand, was in my final destination for today and many more to come if the police wanted to be shitty. Looking out this long, narrow window depressed me a great deal. But still, it didn't measure up to the way I felt when I looked around this small, concrete cell instead of out that window. Only twenty –four hours in and I was completely disgusted with the writing on the walls, the limited amount of space, thin ass foam mattress, and top ramen noodles. Fuck this shit! Oh and did I mention my cellie is a fat stankin' ass bitch that has a serious hygiene problem but always wanna hug and high five blowin' that hot ass breath all throughout the cell. Every time she looked as if she was gonna open her mouth I covered my nose with the collar of my shirt and wanted to knock fire from her ass. I didn't kill Bianca but murder just might stick when I kill this bitch.

"Flower! Let's go you have a visit," the correctional officer said as she approached my cell. Standing to my feet, I fixed my clothes and headed to the bars to be handcuffed before being escorted to my visit. As we walked down the tier I caught a glimpse of all the strange and unfriendly stares given by my fellow inmates. Common sense told me it was all because it was a rule of the game. But frustration said it was because they wanted me to reach out and touch they ass with these hands. Either way I was handcuffed and couldn't do anything if they paid me to. The steel, double sided elevator was huge and cold on the inside; so cold that my body began to shiver almost immediately after we entered. When the door opposite of our entry came open I was lead to a room that looked much better than the last. Its tile was clean and shining as if they waxed the floor, the table was big and resembled an activity desk at a pre-school; the walls were in perfect shape; no writing or filth. As I looked around the room I thought, "Wow, they done stepped their game up." After about two minutes Detective Banks walked in the room smiling like the Kool-Aid man. Another detective, that I never seen, accompanied him. "Ms. Flower," he said looking down at the table like he was thinking about something then back up at me, "How are you doing today?" Detective Banks could care less about how I was doin' so I didn't entertain his ass at all. I gave a sarcastic smile and left it at that.

"Okay. Maybe you'll talk to me about the gun we found in your apartment. You know, the one you had hiding in the closet." I just shook my head and laughed at him. He was tryin' so hard to get a reaction outta me, but nothin' worked. When he pulled the plastic Zip-loc out of the brown paper bag and placed it on the table my blood began to boil. It was written all over my face and he was waitin' on me to react. Why isn't that gun in its box, I thought to myself. If they so much as get a scratch on it I'm gonna kill their ass. This is the one thing I had left of my grandmother. "We found your little stash. Now we need to hear your story on where you got it and why you got it." I still said nothin' in response to his statement and since I planned on exercisin' my right to remain silent each and every time I was questioned, this interview went nowhere. They were in the same predicament today that they were in almost two days ago. And for those reasons I was taken back to my cell.

Since the gun was found in my aunt's room, hadn't been used in years, and was registered to my grandmother, the police were really mad when they had to release me and watch me walk out of those double doors. My aunt was pissed about them raiding the house and just as I thought, Shawna went ballistic. But both of them were happy to see me free again. On the ride home they filled me in on everything that has happened in my absence.

Chapter Seven

2 1/2 Months Later....

As time went on, goin' to jail and catchin' enemies slippin' became more and more irrelevant. I had even begun to feel better about the situation with Matt. The past couple of months I been on the grind, makin' this money, and preparing for my next move. If Matt thinks I just one day woke up stupid, he was in for a surprise. Soon as I could, I'm gone show his ass my real get down.

In the two short months Matt had been gone, I managed to crack a spot, begin the process of opening another, and stack $15,000. My shit was crump tight and doing very well, all without him knowing a thing. To ensure things stayed that way, about two weeks before he came home I hired a couple of workers to maintain the spot while I wasn't there. When Matt came home to see me still waiting on him hand and foot, loving him the same and not an attitude the first, he really thought he was the man. His pride and self-confidence shot through the roof. Me on the other hand, I was like a hawk. My ass knew everything he did, where he was at, and who he was with. I was too fly and too strong to sit around nagging so I kept it calm and quiet. I mean a real fuckin' lady about my shit.

Weeks later, here I was still doin' me. Still, Matt didn't notice a thing. The streets had been good to me. But now was the time to rip these muthafuckas up.

"Alright, babe. I'll see you later." Matt said leaning down to give me a kiss.

"Okay, babe. Where you goin'?"

"I'm goin' wit' Kay for a little while."

"Oh, alright."

Kay my ass! I thought to myself. How he goin' wit Kay and his ass at home cupcakin' wit' his bitch? Niggas and the games they play. But, that's okay. I got a couple of runs to make myself. The spot on 102nd was poppin' today. Jack done already called me sayin' he needed some work, so I picked that up and slid by there to do a swap.

"What up Jack," I asked as I entered the spot using my key.

"What's crackin' KeKe," he responded with a head nod.

"Shit, I can't call it. Here's the work. Make sure you put this shit up though."

As he reached over the counter to grab the work he said, "Alright," and proceeded to put the work in the stash. Not even thirty minutes after I got there my phone started ringin'.

"Talk."

Ay, KeKe! Where you at wit' it?"

"At work. Why? What up?"

"Yo man!"

"Oh yeah? What about 'em?"

"He over here booed up wit' some bitch. She 'bout to leave though so hurry up."

Without another word I hung up the phone and told Jack to hold it down. After jumping in my car it took me all of two minutes to pull up on his ass. I was on 93rd knockin' on the door ready to give him a rude awakening.

"Who is it?"

"KeKe!"

Silence flooded the air as I stood at the door. No one else uttered a word. Knocking again, this time harder than the last, I yelled, "Open the door I gotta pee!"

"Hold up. I'm trying to find the key," T Ray yelled.

The dead bolt lock on the front door only permitted entrance with a key. Normally, I would have the key, but since I didn't have plans on comin' by here today I left it at home. Standing outside, I took a mental note of all the cars parked in front, realizing it was only one car out here that didn't belong.

"Ay KeKe, Cuz! You gon' have to come through the back 'cause I can't find it," he finally yelled through the door.

As I made my way around back, walking down the catwalk that trailed through a group of neatly trimmed bushes leading to the back, something stopped me dead in my tracks. I'm not sure what it was but I had a gut feeling that this was a set-up. Something about this wasn't right. Standing at the side of the house, quiet as a church-mouse, I noticed a female running from the direction of the front door and to her car. Just as I assumed, the Hondai hatch-back was hers. Determined to show this nigga my true get-down, I sprang into action, running toward her. By the time I made it to her car, she was already in it, trying to start it up. With the windows up and doors locked my only option was to try and kick the window out.

BAM!...BAM!...BOOM!

BRIDGE 2 DESTRUCTION

After three tries I was all in. I kicked the fuck out of that window sending shattered glass flying everywhere. With a handful of hair, I tried snatching that bitch up out of the car only to be unsuccessful. She screeched off down Broadway fast as hell. By this time everybody on the block was standing outside looking, but still, I wanted my prey. I ran to my car, jumped in, and... Nothing. Over and over again I got nothin'.

"Fuck!" I screamed hittin' the steering wheel with tears flowing down my face. I was angry as hell and badly wanted to release my anger. With nothin' left to do but enter the spot I did so and found Matt dumb ass in there wit' his belt unbuckled trying to throw on some shoes.

"Bitch-ass nigga! This the shit you playin'? Well I hope yo' ass is ready cause I'mma tear some shit up every muthafuckin' time. Yo' dumb ass don't want a good bitch, you want an ignorant one so I'mma be that. Oh yeah, bitch, I'm gon' be that."

"Get yo' ass outta here wit' that shit. How you know she was over here wit' me?"

Not wanting to expose my source I thought of somethin' quick. "You the only dumb ass nigga in here tryin' to get dressed. Not to mention I'm not fuckin' wit' neither one of these niggas," I said pointing to the two guys that occupied the room, "so they don't have no reason not to let me in or have their bitch run up outta here."

"Man, look. I just woke up. I don't know what the fuck you talkin' about."

"Okay that's cool. But watch this bitch. Watch this," I said storming out of the house and back to my car.

Out of all the time I had this car it has never stalled on me. Now all of a sudden, on today of all days, it gives me a problem. Jumpin' in my car I gave the key another turn but got nothin'. When I popped the hood everything looked fine but the twist of one of the cables verified the problem. It was loose. Once I tightened it, I jumped back in and it fired right up. *Ain't this a bitch*, I thought to myself. Before I could pull off, Matt comes outside tryin' to show his ass. Now here was the part I was waitin' on. After all we been through, I never, and I mean never, showed my ass in public. Today would definitely prove to be different. I played misses nice bitch for way too long. As he approached my car wit that bullshit I hopped out and started swingin'. Everything in me knew I better not stop because when and if I did he was really gonna fuck me up. Like Tyson and Holyfield, we got it in. Cars were pullin' over tryin' to get a glimpse of what was goin' on, but no one broke it up. They just enjoyed having front row seats to see the fight of the day. Blows were bein' thrown all in the middle of Broadway and neither one of us gave a shit about who seen it. Catching a powerful blow to the mouth, I grabbed my mouth allowing blood to seep through my fingers. The sight of blood had me vexed.

"You want me to call the police?" an older white woman asked holdin' her cellphone.

"Hell naw!" I said releasing my hand from my mouth, almost completely out of breath, bouncin' side to side like I was in the ring. "I got this."

No sooner than those words left my mouth the police came driving up the block and pulled over to try and get the crowd to disburse. Bogarding their way through the crowd, the police officer approached me trying to find out what the problem was. Matt disappeared in the crowd opposite of their approach.

"Ma'am what's going on here?" the tall, lanky ass cop asked with one hand on his waist belt and the other down at his side.

"Nothin'" I responded dryly with fire in my eyes, still kinda maintainin' my rhythm.

"I think you're lying. You look like you were fighting." As if his words were of no interest to me I just looked at him and didn't say a word.

"Who were you fighting?"

Still I stayed silent and slowly turned and walked away makin' my way to my car.

"Ma'am I can't help you if you don't tell me what happened. You want EMT to take a look at that cut on your mouth," he spoke a tad bit louder than before due to my walking away.

"No I'm cool. I gotta go," I yelled back to him still moving forward. With that said I hopped in my car and pulled off.

When I got home, Matt wasn't there. There was exactly one hour left before time to pick up Mai from school so I cleaned my face and applied ice to my lip. This shit is crazy. Never in a million years did I think I would ever go through some shit like this wit' him, I thought to myself. And I couldn't help but wonder what he was thinkin' at this moment. Regardless of what I was feelin' I knew for a fact he probably couldn't believe I went there wit his ass. There was a lot more comin' where that came from though. It would be a flat out lie if I said I didn't love him because I did. But the shit that unraveled before my eyes the past few months had kinda hardened my heart. It made me downplay those loving and caring actions of mines and wanna replace them with revenge.

Chapter Eight

Although Matt had fucked up on more than one occasion I remained his Bonnie in the streets and played my position at home. We had our share of trials and tribulations but still I stayed with him. Most of my time was spent handling business in the streets or hangin' out wit Mai. He never really knew really knew my whereabouts and I never bothered to question his. I wasn't about to stress over it. Everything revealed itself in due time so I just waited for them days to come and let my actions speak for me. Showin' my ass in the streets was becoming a big part of me and from start to finish Matt never saw it comin'.

BRIDGE 2 DESTRUCTION

Ring! Ring!

"Talk!"

"KeKe! Where you at Cuz?"

"I'm in traffic right now, why? You need that?"

"Hell yeah and I got a little game for you to play too."

"That's what's up. I'll be there in ten. No! Make it thirty minutes. I gotta go grab somethin' to eat. I'm hungry as hell."

"All yo' ass do is eat KeKe, damn! That's why that ass so big."

"Shut up stupid! Bye."

Baby Cash always had somethin' stupid comin' outta his mouth. But I loved him. He was wit the business and loyal to the game. That's why I fucked wit' 'em. If there were any young niggas left in the game worth trusting, Baby Cash was definitely one of them. Having served two jail sentences for some shit he didn't do and havin' a body count higher than the morgue, I would say Baby Cash had more than proved his loyalty to the game. Plus, his young ass has been havin' a crush on me ever since I was in Jr. High school and he was in elementary.

As promised I pulled up to the spot with a few minutes hangin'. With a gym bag in one hand, my soda and keys in the other, and my bag of food hangin' from my mouth, I kicked the door for him to come open it.

"Who is it?" he yelled.

Unable to speak, I kicked the door one more time.

"Aw shit KeKe," he said opening the door after noticing it was me. "Why you didn't just ask for some help?"

Sitting my soda and keys on the table then releasing the bag from my mouth I said, "Because I didn't need no help. Now, here goes your shit" I said sliding him the gym bag, "and, here goes my shit" referring to the bag of food I had just dropped on the table.

"See this is what I'm talkin' 'bout," Baby Cash said comin' face to face wit' the two snow white pouches of dope in the gym bag.

"Alright I ain't got all day so slide me my funds and get to talkin' 'bout this game you got up," I said, talking with a mouth full of food.

"Okay! Peep! It's this dude named Ocho that's supposed to be the man out there in Colorado. I'm not sure yet if he's connected to our empire but I already got somebody lookin' into it. Anyway, he had to relocate out here for a little while, while things cool down out there. Word around town is he's lookin for a female friend."

"Is that right? And why would I want that friend to be me?"

"'Cause we can come up. Don't act like you ain't wit' the stick up game Cuz."

"Okay. You're right. What can you tell me about him?"

"So far this is what I got. His real name is Darius Byron. He's forty-five years old, no kids, deceased wife, and oh yeah, sittin' on about two mills," he said smiling.

Pleased with him doin' his homework, I nodded my head in satisfaction.

"Don't smile at me like that. Like you just know two mill is gonna make me jump into action."

"Cuz, what! Yo ass know you gon' get this nigga," Baby Cash said laughing.

"I know huh. Naw but, you did a good job on that homework my Nig. One mo' question though."

"Shoot."

"How did his wife die?"

"Some say she was killed in a robbery gone bad, but others say he killed her. I really don't care who killed the bitch. Wit two mill all I care about is who gone kill his bitch ass."

"Yeah I feel you. But the answer to that question can tell you a lot about him. So find that out. What's the plan?"

"Basically I want us to rob the nigga," Baby Cash said pumped and as-a-matter-of-factly.

I looked at him with my eyebrows lifted and said, "That's it?" and he just stood there.

"That ain't no plan fool!"

Grabbing my money off the table that he placed there while talkin' to me, along with my soda and keys, I said, "Call me when you got a real plan. A plot and a plan is two different things my nigga. Learn the difference before you start fuckin' wit' the big fish 'cause it sounds to me like yo' plan is to die or get me killed."

I looked into his eyes for a few seconds to show him I was serious and without another word I walked away and got into my car. Two more drop offs and I'm free to relax. The second stop was to Shawna. Her ghetto ass was still doin' her thang but had graduated to the dope game. She still had the same spot and everything. When I pulled up and seen that candy painted Lexus all I could do was smile. I was proud of my cuzo and happy to see that leavin' her that spot wasn't a big mistake. When I honked the horn she came outside sporting a special made jumpsuit complimented by some Doonie & Burke sandals and a big purse to match. You couldn't tell by the way she dressed that she was ghetto but when she opened her mouth confirmation came.

"Ahh! What up Bi-otch? Ha you doin'," she said loud as fuck and smacking the shit outta that gum, she continued talkin'. "KeKe, where ma lil cuzin' at girl cause I need to see her."

"What up Shawna," I laughed shaking my head. "Mai is at school tryin' to learn somethin'. And why yo' ass so loud? When you talk to me you gon' have to whisper. I can't say use yo' inside voice cause ever since we were little girls that has been yo' inside voice."

"Fuck you Cuz!" she said while I placed the two zips in her purse and retrieved the money it held.

"Call me later. I got another run to make. I love you."

"I love you too bitch. Bye!"

I need some move music, I said to myself after placing the money in my bag. Rambling through all the cd's I finally came to a mixed cd. When I popped it in the first song to come on was my shit.

Slow down / I just wanna get to know you / but don't turn around / cause that pretty round thang looks good to me... Bobby Valentino was bumping out the sound system. Song after song I got my groove on while driving under the AC. As I pulled up to my last stop I noticed Matt's ass pullin' out of the driveway. What the hell was he doin' over here? I questioned myself out loud. Not wanting to go there at the moment I pretended I didn't see him and didn't care. My money was more important at the moment. As routine I honked my horn and Joy's fat ass came runnin' out.

"Hey KeKe! What's up?"

She showed no signs of nervousness or anything. Everything was real copasetic.

"Shit makin' this money. What's up wit' you?"

"The same thang," she said slidin' me the money.

"Who all over here?"

"Just my little sister and some of the home girls."

"Alright well y'all have a good one. Be careful," I said meaning every word of it. I made a mental note of what I had just seen and planned on lookin' into it a little further. Lord knows I don't need any more drama in my life but I wouldn't be right until I knew what was goin' on.

Back at the house he acted as if nothing was wrong. Either he didn't see me or he did see me and didn't wanna make it obvious.

"Hi Babe!" he said kissing me on the forehead.

"What's up? What you doin' home?"

"About to get dressed and go hook up wit Kay."

Kay was his all-time favorite alibi. He could be in a whole nother state and would still find a way for Kay to be his alibi.

"You just got here?" I asked to see if he was gon' lie and he did.

"Naw. I been in the house all day. That's why I ain't got dressed yet."

I laughed so hard inside it wasn't funny. But now I know without a doubt he didn't see me 'cause he would have come with somethin' better than that for sure.

With over an hour left before I had to pick up Mai, I decided to give Matt a pass and take a nap.

Chapter Nine

With Mai over to my sister's house and Matt in the streets I finally had time to count my funds. Once the bottom drawer of the dresser was pulled out I was able to release the hand-made box that was underneath and attached to the drawer just above it. When I placed it on the bed it was like a blank to my eyes. It felt good to see that I was back on my shit and doing pretty good. Five-thousand-six-hundreddollars, that's cool I thought to myself. Add that to the fifteen racks I already had and it was a lovely twenty-thousand-six-hundred dollars. Business was cool and Matt's time was tickin'. While he played Rollin' stone, his well was about to run dry. And when it did, that would be all she wrote. His ass was gon' look stupid as fuck because he lost a down ass bitch over fuckin' wit' bitches that couldn't do shit but suck or sit on a dick.

Ring!Ring!..

"Talk."

"Damn I hate the way you answer your phone KeKe," my sister Kai said irritated as hell.

"What's up sis? You ready for me to come get Mai?"

"No actually I'm callin' to see if she can stay. My niece don't wanna go home tonight."

"Alright that's cool wit' me. She got clothes over there and her hair is braided so she's cool."

"Alright well, we'll see you tomorrow."

"Alright sis, make sure you give her a kiss for me and tell her I love her."

"Alright I will."

"Okay. Bye!"

"Ke!" she yelled in the phone.

"What up?"

"Did you now Matt and Bo was goin' out to the club together tonight?"

"Naw. He told me he was goin' somewhere wit' Kay. I guess we'll see how it goes down huh."

Kai was mad. For some reason she believed everything Bo said and held on to his every word. Not me! The only thing I believed out of Matt's mouth was his name. In the beginning everything was everything. Now, all he do is lie.

After ending the call with Kai I decided to go hit a few corners myself. With no particular destination in mind I drove until finally I was at the beach. The thought of looking out at the water and bright stars shining above me, kinda eased my mind. As I entered the darkest cul-de-sac adjacent to the beach I felt an immediate sense of anxiousness. Finally, I can relax I thought to myself as I swiftly made way toward the water. My mind wandered into space, blocking out all the drama and negativity in my life, and bringing me to a place of calmness and relaxation. Looking out into the water I wondered where it would lead me. How different it would be living over there. And what if I just got up and left right now.

Before long, a smile spread across my face and my spirit was at peace. I marveled over the way the water sounded as it hit hard against the rocks. The soft breeze sent my hair blowing in the wind like I was auditioning for an outdoor photo shoot. The mist combined with the light fog moistened my skin leaving a dampness that sent chills through my body. It was so enjoying that I found myself lost in a world of my own. Time must have flown by because before I knew it, it was approaching two in the morning. On my way to the car my phone blew up. It rung on at least five different occasions before I decided to pay it any mind. The caller ID said it was Kai. What the hell could she want at 2 a.m.?

"Talk. I mean, what's up?"

"Have you talked to Matt cause Bo still ain't came home and he ain't answering his phone."

"Girl I don't be on Matt like that but if I talk to him I'll let you know. I have to call you back."

Not leaving her another chance to go all crazy on the phone I hung up and tried starting my car. When it fired up, I let it warm up for a minute as I listened to Sade on the Wave. First the water, then Sade, my night was getting better and better. As Sade's song ended I exited the parking lot and hit the 10fwy. Not too far from the beach my car started driving funny so I pulled to the shoulder to see what was up. Before I popped my hood I turned off the engine and hit the hazards, somethin' I shouldn't have done because it refused to start back up. AAA was the first thing that came to mind but after fumbling through my purse, even that was a no go due to me leaving the card in my other purse when I switched it this morning. Kai was at home wit the kids, Matt wasn't answering his phone, and neither was anyone else.

Finally a car came pulling up parking a few feet ahead of me. I couldn't see him too well from the distance but I did know he was tall and dressed in all white. I needed his help badly but I wasn't about to be the dumb bitch that got kidnapped, raped, and killed by a nigga who picked me up off the freeway. I leaned over in my car, retrieving my .380 from its stash and placed it at my side. As the strange man had gotten closer to me I examined him with my eyes, from head to toe. This nigga was F-I-N-E! The ice white linen suit he wore complimented his chocolate skin. He was clean cut, with the body of a football player and the walk of a certified G. You know the one that's smooth but bold and dared a nigga to run up.

"You need any help young lady?" he asked revealing a perfect set of beautiful white teeth.

"Um. Naw, I'm cool. My boyfriend should be on his way," I lied.

"Boyfriend huh? A beautiful young lady like you should have a husband."

"Whatever!" I said trying to conceal the smile that was anxiously wanting to form across my face.

"You sure you don't want my help? It's late and kinda cold out here."

"I'm cool. I don't even know you." I told him not wanting to give in too easy.

"Okay well, Hi! My name is Dee. And you are?" he asked stretching out his arm to shake my hand.

"Shawn." I said placing my hand inside his only to feel the softness of his lips instead of a firm handshake.

"Nice to meet you beautiful. Now we know each other. Can I help you now?"

"I still don't know you. How I know you not gon' try to kill me or somethin'? I know you think that little kiss on the hand was real smooth but come on. Be for real! Ain't no knight-in-shining-armors waiting to save no princesses in the ghetto."

Dee looked at me and burst out laughing. "You ain't lyin' about that. Just let me take you home and you can handle the rest in the morning."

"Alright," I said giving in. "But let me let you know right now, I know Tai Kwan Do and I got a cold right hook. If you make one wrong move I'ma knock yo' fine ass out."

Dee laughed again and shook his head, "I don't know how or where I found you at," he said playfully.

"I do! You found my little innocent ass stuck on the side of the freeway while you were out canvasing the highway lookin' for somebody to kill."

Once again, Dee started laughing. "Yo' man got it bad wit' you. I can tell."

"And how can you tell that? Wait! Don't tell me yo' ass is psychic too. That's probably how you knew I was out there."

"No I'm not psychic. I can tell 'cause you don't take other people's feelings into consideration when you talk. Here I am offering to help you and you done insulted me, threatened me, and disrespected me."

"Wait! How I disrespect you?"

"By callin' another nigga yo' boyfriend while your man is standin' right here."

No longer able to conceal my smile, I revealed it to him, big enough for the world to see. Our whole conversation consisted of sarcasm and laughter. We both enjoyed the ride back to my hood and looked forward to talking again soon. Through all the laughs and smiles I still did as I knew I should. Instead of allowing him to take me home I played his ass into thinking smoked-out ass Diane's house was mines. Exiting the car, I said my good-byes and he made me promise to call him later in the day. Thank God Diane lived only two blocks from me. As soon as his car disappeared into the night I hoped her back gate then cut through the apartment complex that led to my house. Surprisingly not, Matt's ass still wasn't here. In a way it was good because I could enjoy the smile that's spread across my face as a result of the episodes of today.

Chapter Ten

Before my alarm could wake me up my phone had rung, beating it to the punch. Damn I'm tired of this phone. I purposely ignored the last two calls but whoever this was, wasn't gonna stop callin'. Today wasn't even one of those days that I had to get up early, so when I did answer, I nearly jumped through the phone on their ass.

"What the fuck..."

"KeKe, it's me!"

"Kai? Girl what you want this early in the mornin'?" I really didn't care and wanted to just hang up the phone but it just felt like the right question to ask.

"Bo didn't come home," she said cryin' hysterically. "He ain't never did this shit before. What if somethin' happened to him?"

"Kai, baby calm down. Ain't nothin' happened to him. And before you ask me how I know, call his phone. If the muthafucka ring you know he cool 'cause he had sense enough to charge that muthafucka up wherever he at."

To Kai that made a lot of sense but she still wasn't letting me off the phone. She dialed Bo's number on three-way and just like I said, it rung its way to the voicemail. In a snap her tears had stopped and she flipped into ignorant mode.

"This nigga got me fucked up. Come get me KeKe so we can bend some corners."

"*You* go bend some corners! *I'm* goin' back to sleep. When I get up if you still want to get out in the streets, we will."

My choice of words must have pissed her off 'cause she hung up in my face. It didn't last long though because just as I was drifting into deep sleep my phone rang again, non-stop.

"KeKe get yo' ass up, I know where they at," Kai yelled in the phone.

Lookin' at the clock I seen I had been sleep for almost two hours since her last call. "Okay where they at?"

"At some house on 66th and Menlo. I don't know the exact house but that's where they are," she said.

And the games begin, I thought to myself. "Here I come Kai, be ready when I get there."

The ride to Kai's house was quiet and held no thought. My mind was already set on fuckin' some shit up so why waste time thinking or stressin' over it?

Once Kai was in the car, that silence had changed into loud threats and promises. Baby went off the whole way there, to the point where I wanted to duct tape he mouth closed. When we pulled up on 66th we scanned the houses and driveways for anything familiar. Nothing caught our eyes but I had a gut feelin' it was the brown house that sat two houses from the corner on our left. While sittin' down the street doin' our stake out, we discussed different ways to find out if this was in fact the house. Then suddenly it hit me. Out of all the houses on the block this one was poppin'. The music was bumpin' and you could hear people on the inside, laughing and talking shit. That's what made me focus in on this particular house.

"Kai!" I turned in my seat to face her. "How about we go to that payphone right there and call 'em. If they answer and we hear that same music in the background we know we're right."

"Good idea. Come on let's go."

Picking up the phone, which was located at the next corner, I dialed Matt's number.

"Hello!" he answered, soundin' all pumped and excited.

"Baby, where you at?" I asked as if everything was cool. Out of nowhere, he starts whisperin' and shushing people in the background. Even the music was turned down a bit.

"I'm on my way home. Why?"

"You still think this is a game huh? Watch this! We gone see who is pumped and excited after this. You were better off not answerin' the phone, stupid!" With those final words I hung up the phone.

"What happen?" Kai asked.

"He's in there, and we 'bout to be in there too. Female intuition is a muthafucka ain't it?"

Excited to finally show her ass and snatch her nigga up by the collar, Kai smiled and rubbed her hands together. "Let's do this!"

By the time we made it back down the street it was quiet as hell. The music was off, the door was closed, and the blinds were closed. None of that stopped me from knocking on the door though. With every knock my blood began to boil. My adrenaline was rushing to the point that my right leg began to shake. No one answered. The sound of something fallin' over verified someone was still in there. I knocked again, still no answer. Tired of the shenanigans, I looked to Kai and whispered, "You ready?" She had no idea what I was about to do but still she nodded yeah and I made my move.

"Ahhhh!"

Screams poured out of the mouths of the females inside the house as the chair that once occupied the porch, came flying through the huge picture window in the living room. Retrieving my gun from my waistline and now inside the house, I unlocked the door for Kai to enter. No one was in the living room however we did catch two of them in what appeared to be the family room, which was the next room over.

"Hahaha! Y'all crazy Cuz." Bo laughed as he exited the house firing up a cigarette, walking slowly toward the front porch.

"Oh it's funny bitch?" Kai spat at Bo as he walked past her as if he hadn't did anything wrong. Clearly Bo was high off of somethin' but Kai failed to acknowledge it. She was past pissed off and needed to prove a point.

"We gone see how funny it-is," she said pausing as she popped him upside the back of da head, "when I whoop this bitch ass."

Bo looked at Kai through piercing eyes and wanted desperately to slap da shit outta her but didn't because the truth of the matter was, he was wrong. Not to mention her retarded ass sister was here and he didn't have time to deal wit the extras that came along wit her fuck-a-nigga attitude.

"Which one of you hoes is fuckin' wit' him?" Kai asked the two girls who were now layin' faced down on the floor at gun point. Neither of them said a word and Kai got furious, kicking the one closest to her in the head.

"Oh so now you bitches can't hear?"

"Hold up killa! Let me go through the rest of this house before you do your shit."

I searched room after room, ordering the two bitches I found hiding in the shower to go lay it down wit their friends on the family room floor. When asked where Matt was, nobody claimed to know a thing. It pissed me off more and more but I remained calm. There was one door left. When I turned the knob it was locked. With the butt of the gun I knocked on the door taunting whoever sat on the other side of that door. "Come out. Come out, whoever you are," I sung like a kid playin' hide-and-go-seek, but no one answered.

"I ain't got time for the games so open this fuckin' door," I yelled demandingly. Still, no one answered. "I'm gon' count to three and if this muthafuckin' door don't open I'ma shoot this muthafucka up!"

"One....... Two...."

"Wait! Please don't," a female cried from behind the door after hearing my gun cock, "my kids are in here."

Just as quick as she finished her plea the door swung open. Looking around the room I saw the two kids, one was a newborn and the other looked to be about five.

"Where is Matt at?" I asked the half-naked, hysterical female. Crying crocodile tears she said, "He left out the back door."

"Oh okay! So you the bitch he fuckin' wit'," I said more like a statement than a question. She just shook her head in agreement and when she did, the butt of my .380 sent her frail, ugly ass flyin' across the room and into the closet door. Her oldest daughter cried in fear and covered her face with a teddy bear.

"The only reason I ain't gon' shoot yo' bitch ass is because of these kids. You better thank God fo' their ass. And you might wanna stop fuckin' niggas around them too wit' yo' dumb ass," I said walking away joining Kai in the family room.

"You ready?" I asked her.

"Wait."

BOOM! BOOM!

She shot the two females that she exchanged words with upon entry in the house, both in the head and said, "Now I'm ready," fixing her clothes like she was that bitch.

"Okay sis, I see you," I said smiling and nodding my head in approval.

By this time Bo was long gone and his whereabouts were unknown. Kai didn't give a fuck as long as her point was proven and it was. On the way home, I questioned Kai about what had just happened.

"Where was the other two girls that I sent in there?"

"What two girls?"

Pulling over to the curbside of the next street, I threw the car in park and looked at her. "You mean to tell me that nobody else came and laid they ass down on that floor while I was in the back of the house?"

"Nope."

"Fuck! Them bitches got out the back door. I bet you they did. I didn't know it had one until I talked to that other bitch though."

"Well now we definitely got a problem. We don't even know who the fuck they are."

Irritated by the whole situation, I put the car back in drive and continued thinking about how bad this could go. Kai had just killed two people, I left a witness because of her kids, and two more witnesses escaped out the back door. "I gotta fix this Cuz, ASAP."

~$~

Later that evening, Bo was at home, front and center with dinner cooked and all. Kai sat smiling, thinkin' to herself, "Yeah fall in line nigga 'cause you fuckin' wit' a boss."

Chapter Ten

After all that happened today I needed time to chill out. Looking at my phone I noticed I had quite a few missed calls. When checking my messages three of them were from D.

"Hey sweetie give me a call." Message erased... next message.

"Hey beautiful this is D. I wanna make sure everything is okay wit' yo ride. Call me back." Message erased... next message.

"I'm leaving to go OT tonight, hit me so I can see you before I leave." Message erased... there are no more messages.

I guess it wouldn't hurt to call him. With all the drama and chaos in my life, I'm sure it couldn't get any worse. Besides, he's the person that actually put a smile on my face and right about now I wouldn't mind another one. Scrolling down the missed call list I came to his number and pressed TALK. It rung and rung, and just as I began to hang up the phone a deep voice full of excitement said, "Hello!"

Putting the phone back to my ear I said, "Hey, this is Shawn."

"Oh hey, I didn't think you were gonna call."

"Why? Cause I didn't call you first thing this morning like the rest of your little groupies?"

"Naw actually I doubted you because I know the games you women have to play when you have a boyfriend."

"Oh do you? And I suppose next you're gonna say you're different."

"Damn right I am. That's why I'm classified as a man or potential husband. Not no damn boyfriend."

"I heard the fuck outta that!"

"So can I see you today? My flight leaves at 6 a.m. tomorrow and I would love to at least have dinner with you tonight."

"And where exactly do you plan on takin' me for dinner?"

"My house. I'll be your personal chef."

"You still tryin' to kill me huh? Not only do you wanna lure me to your house but you wanna poison me too? That's fucked up," I said sadly, as if my feelings were really hurt. D laughed and said, "I could have killed yo little ass last night if I wanted to. You ain't no bigger than a minute."

Smiling myself, I responded, "Yeah, I might be little but you didn't know what I was workin' wit' and probably didn't wanna risk another car pullin' up seein' you get yo big ass whooped by little ole me. Now you want me to come to your house so you could have home court advantage? Trust me, the scene might change but the outcome remains the same bruh."

By now D was bustin' up laughin'. Our make believe fights was enough to soothe the both of us. It was a connection or vibe that came natural.

"You are somethin' else."

"I know."

"So can a brotha please have the privilege of takin' you out before I go?" he asked a little more serious than before.

"Sure you can. I would love to go to dinner with you."

"Great! I'll pick you…."

"Hold up. Hold up. Hold up," I said cutting him off before he could finish his statement, "I'll meet you wherever you want but you ain't pickin' me up from nowhere. I still don't know you like that."

"Okay I see you gon' be a tough one. But anything worth havin' is definitely worth fightin' for."

That statement alone won me over because most men fail to realize that. I laid there, on my queen-sized bed blushing and twirling my feet, feelin' like I had a childhood crush. After about fifteen minutes we agreed on a meeting place and I had one hour to get it together. To keep me in the perfect mood I popped a CD into the CD player and jumped in the shower.

Music Soul child's *B.U.D.D.Y.* escaped from the speakers setting the tone as I grooved in the shower. Song after song, I sang and twirled my body to the beat while I dried off, lotioned up, dressed, and did my hair. Exactly forty-five minutes later I was a beautiful masterpiece ready to hit the streets and show off the woman I rarely displayed. With all the drama and chaos from Matt and these streets, cute was all I could display. Now that a new acquaintance and a new surrounding had presented itself I was gonna greet it lookin' nothin' less than fly. To compliment my style I decided to drive my Lexus. When I fired it up Lucy Pearls, *Dance Tonight*, was on the radio assisting me in maintaining my groove. The coolness of the night seeped through the cracks left in my two rear windows causing me to shiver with chills.

As I drove through the city streets I thought of the smiles D put on my face and how good it felt. With all the deception, lies, and drama presented throughout my life, I almost forgot that a genuine smile felt this good.

After valet parking and walking through the double doors of Joe's Crab Shack, I found D already seated at the table awaiting my arrival. The mere sight of him put an even bigger smile on my face. Moving towards the table, I slowly removed my jacket to reveal my grown and sexy sense of style and he stood to his feet to embrace me. His firm yet sensual hold around me sent a message to my heart that said, *now this is how things are supposed to be.* When he released me from his hold he planted a soft kiss on my cheek and helped me to my seat. Pulling my chair out for me was far from reality in my current relationship. I'd be lucky if Matt allowed me to have a seat before him. So when he did that, I exposed another smile.

"Aw, thank you."

"You're welcome," he said taking his seat directly across from me.

"What are you smiling so much for?"

"Because you came. And let's not forget to mention, you *are* beautiful."

"Don't be tryin' to butter me up. You don't know me like that." He smiled and threw his hands up like he was defeated.

Dinner was delicious. The Barbeque Dungeness crab legs were the business and the margaritas were excellent. We chilled and talked like two friends that had known each other forever. Just as dinner was about to come to an end, D scooted his chair close to mines, placed my hands inside his, and asked, "Shawn is it okay to see each other more often? I mean I know we just met but I'm diggin' you and I would love to see what lies ahead of us."

"Well D, I'm in a very complicated situation right now and starting another relationship is the last thing on my mind right now. Don't get me wrong, I like talkin' to you but not for that reason."

"That's fair. But do me a favor. Think about it. I'll be gone for a week or so but I'll call you. And when I come back we'll see how you feel then."

"Okay but don't get your hopes up." I said to him as I stood to my feet and put my coat on.

Seeing this conversation had definitely come to an end D left the money for the tab and a twenty dollar tip on the table and proceeded to follow me out to the parking lot. The valet attendant accepted our tickets and ordered the drivers to go retrieve the cars. Within minutes one of the drivers pulled up in a dark blue Cadillac STS with limo-tented windows and sittin' on some twenty inch chrome Cadillac rims. When the driver door opened Teddy Pendergrass's Turn out the lights, could be heard loud and smooth.

With the door closed nothing could be heard, as if the car was sound proofed or something. Shortly after, the second driver surfaced driving my car, which he pulled right behind D's Cadillac. D and I walked hand in hand to my car and before we parted he kissed my cheek and gave me a single rose which he had gotten from a vendor outside the restaurant.

"Thanks D. Have a safe trip and maybe I'll see you when you get back."

"Oh, you will beautiful."

My car door closed and I disappeared into the night as if I were a ghost.

Chapter Eleven

"KeKe!"

BAM! BAM! BAM!

"KeKe!"

BAM! BAM!

What the fuck? I know a muthafucka is not bamming on my damn door like this early in the goddamn morning. "What!" I yelled as I swung the door open, mad as hell at the disrespectful son-of-a-bitch at the door. Half asleep and completely out of whack, I stared at my visitor rubbing my eyes trying to distinguish who they were through my blurred vision. After pulling myself together I noticed it was the smoker bitch Diane. *Aw, hell naw*, I thought to myself. I know this bitch ain't over here yelling, bamming, and waking me up outta my sleep for no dope. As the bar door came flyin' open Diane defended herself.

"Wait! KeKe, don't start trippin," she said with her hands wide open and both arms stretched out in my direction. "Somebody just shot yo' mama house up."

"What you mean somebody? Did anybody get hit?"

"Somebody! I think everybody is okay but the shooters were in a black truck."

"What kind of black truck," I asked while trying to brush my teeth and fumble for my car keys.

"Like an Explorer or somethin'."

"A'ight good lookin out."

Diane left out the house and hurried down the street. Seconds later, I was out too, locking the door and jumpin' in my wheels that were already running due to the automatic start button being pushed on my alarm remote. My adrenaline was already beginning to build so the coolness of the early morning's air didn't bother me as usual. The sun was beaming down on my platinum paint sending off twinkles and glares as I used that 450 engine power to maneuver through the hood with quickness. My shit could be heard from around the block so when I pulled up, before I could come to a complete stop, my nigga Loc and Baby Cash was in the street ready to go.

"What up KeKe Cuz?" Loc said shakin' my hand.

"What up. What happened?" I asked getting' out of my car walkin' towards the house to make sure everything was alright, and it was.

"Them punk ass Mexicans just came through Cuz. They stopped right here in the front and start lettin' off."

Baby Cash interjected from there, "Me and this nigga Loc was layin' in the living room. When we looked out the window and seen them niggas we grabbed our shit and got off."

"Moms and 'em is straight doe," Loc said.

"Cool. Let's move then," I said to them jumpin' back in my car. "Cash, Imma drop you off to my lil low key, Cuz, and you go do yo' thang. Me and Loc right behind you and we'll meet back up at mom's house."

"A'ight."

In about four minutes I had pulled up at the spot and shot Cash the keys. Once he was in and fired it up, "Be careful my nigga," was my words of choice as I threw up the G and proceeded down the street. Loc and I parked on the outskirts of their hood and decided to walk. We both knew our surroundings like the back of our hand just as well as the best place to catch them fools.

The spot they had on the one way was an easy target. Everybody in there was about to feel what this gang bangin' shit was really about. We took the back street and hopped the gate to approach from the back instead of the front for the whole world to see. Loc took the right while I took the left. I crept down the side of the house as quiet as a church-mouse and camaflouged myself in the bushes. Loc must have spotted his target

BRIDGE 2 DESTRUCTION

'cause the Tech 9 could be heard spittin'. No sooner than it did, the side door to the house flung open and our enemies came runnin' out. Neither one of them appeared to be packin' and both of them thought they were gonna get away. While one attempted to run towards the front of the house, the other ran to the back and met his fate. With perfect timing I emerged from the bushes with a blue rag tied around my face and unloaded a ripple of bullets into his torso. His body sunk down to the pavement in slow motion never losing eye contact with me. His eyes were big, holding a blank stare, while his body grew heavier and heavier ultimately becoming dead weight, literally, on the pavement. While quickly making my way toward the direction of my next victim Loc emerged from the other end of the front yard doing the same. Our last standing enemy seemed to be getting away but with almost perfect aim and two heavy hitting weapons I couldn't see it happening. Loc and I both took aim, standing side by side and let our guns bark. Just as I thought, he was hit. How many times, I'll never know but his body fallin' against the gate, then to the ground was enough confirmation for me.

With our guns still drawn we ran down the alley and made way back to the car. When walking, to the car didn't seem too far. But runnin', shiiiiit. By the time I made it to the car I was tired as hell and outta breath.

"Damn KeKe. You alright my nigga?" Loc laughed, lookin' at me all crazy with his tongue pressed between his teeth.

"Fuck you! You ole big ass nigga. Yeah I'm cool."

Still laughing Loc said, "At least I can breathe my nigga. Yo ass sittin' up getting' money and done got lazy. You can't do this real Crip shit no mo'. Ha Ha Ha."

Loc gets on my nerves. All he does is talk shit. He is yet another one of my mother's kids she done picked up in the streets. He surfaced about a year or two before my brother died and been a part of the family ever since. Since my brother's death we'd became thick as thieves and had developed an unbreakable bond. We kept our personal lives to ourselves but when it came to these streets we shared it all. Like my brother and I once were, Loc and I were the duo the streets hated to see. If him and I were together it meant catastrophe.

Back at the house everything was normal. Shell was in the house sockin' the homies up. My dad and sisters sat around laughing. Everybody that came to this house knew of Shell's outburst and just tried to brace themselves for it. Out of respect, they never hit her back but definitely wanted to. She didn't punch like your average female. Baby was hittin' hard, hard enough to had knocked plenty niggas out. While all this was occurring inside, what unfolded outside caused a big disturbance. The car Cash used to get down was pulled along the curbside of the house next door.

"Cuz, why his dumb ass park the car right by the house. I'mma fuck Cuz up for this dumb shit," Loc yelled pumped with anger.

"Naw hold up Loc, Cuz. BC never did no shit like this. Somethin' not right."

We got closer to the car and realized it had been sprayed. It had to be at least five holes visible from where I was standin'.

"Loc, look Cuz. This muthafucka shot up."

All of his anger turned to concern as he realized what I said was true.

"Fuck! Where my nigga at?" Loc asked lookin' confused, sad, and hurt all at the same time.

No sooner than he asked that, the driver side door opened alarming Loc and I to the point where we drew our weapons. Aimed straight for the car, ready to blow somebody's brain out, I stepped into the street and approached the car on the driver side. Loc took the passenger side.

"Loc! Help me Cuz. Help me!"

My gun hit the pavement as I moved swiftly toward the car to prevent Cash from doin' the same. He was hit and his body was about to fall out of the car onto the asphalt. Now in my arms, Cash spoke to me.

"You gon' be alright my nigga, Fuck!"

Now at my side Loc looked down at Cash and went crazy.

"Hell naw! Hell-muthafuckin-naw!" His foot kicked the car and his hands tightly gripped his head. "Not my nigga Cuz!" Tears fell from his eyes and rage built heavier and heavier in his eyes.

"Help me Loc, Cuz. We gotta get this nigga to the hospital."

"Naw Cuz, take me to NeNe, no hospitals," Cash said.

"I don't think NeNe gon' be able to handle this one Cuz. You need to go to the hospital."

"No!"

Still holdin' him around his chest, Loc grabbed his legs and we carried him to the car. By this time, friends and neighbors were all outside looking in disbelief and shedding tears. Sadness was in the air as we successfully put Cash in the backseat of the car.

"You drive KeKe!" Loc said throwing me his keys.

Seconds later, I fired up the Chevy Tahoe and smashed out. My mind was racing just as fast as I was drivin' and Cash's adrenaline must have been doin' the same cause now he couldn't be still.

"I'm not about to die like this!" Baby Cash said with a frown on his face.

"You muthafuckin' right you ain't," Loc responded. "Come on Cuz, you too hard for that," he confirmed.

Nervous as ever and looking for anything to calm his mind, Loc grabbed the bottle of liquor he had on the seat and took a swig.

"Here nigga drink some of this," he said forcing the liquor up to Cash's mouth and down his throat. Cash drank the liquor and socked his fist into his hand. "Fuck! This shit burnin' the fuck outta me."

"I swear to God I'mma lay a whole lot of niggas down for this. On Movin' Gang!" Loc said still hurting from this whole ordeal.

"Loc, see if you can see where he was shot at."

"Come on BC Cuz, lemme check you out me nig."

"Ahhh! Fuck!" Cash screamed from the pain caused by his movement and the constant pressure of Loc's hands searching his wounded body.

"It's too much blood Cuz. I can't see shit! Hold up, it's one in his side. That's all I can see. Shit!"

"The way that car look he gotta be hit more than one time. Keep checkin'."

Minutes later we arrived at Nene's house. She had already set up a wheelchair in the garage to help us get him in the house. Cash reeked of pain and frustration, verbally releasing his anger with every passing second.

"I can't die Cuz. NeNe!" Her shirt was gripped in his hand and forcefully being pulled to his face, "Don't let me die Cuz. On movin' Cuz, you make sure I walk outta here. You hear me?"

Not wanting to make a promise she couldn't keep but desperately needing him to calm down, NeNe replied, "Yeah. Lay down and let me look at you."

While Cash did as he was told Loc was pacing back and forth mumbling on and on about what he planned to do.

When his feet finally stopped moving he said, "Let's go KeKe! NeNe, call us when you're done and let us know the deal. It's time to go play."

And we did just that. For hours we went from drive-by's to jumpin' outta bushes on niggas. It soothed our spirit but it didn't take away the pain. After our final mission I was confident we were going home and Baby Cash was heavy on my mind. Once calmed down and on the road, I checked my phone and had two messages from NeNe. NeNe called Loc.

"I guess she finished."

"Cool. Ask her when can I talk to my nigga."

"Hello. What's the deal?" I asked NeNe confident that all was well.

"Tell her to tell my nigga we did our shit. Don't trip," Loc said smiling and still pumped.

My sudden silence and change of my facial expression spoke volumes. Loc shook his head in disbelief and started socking the dashboard and screaming viciously with anger. My heart had sunk to my feet. Those same words I heard when my brother passed, was repeated to me again with sadness. "He gone!" Unable to speak, I hung up the phone and laid my head on the steering wheel, with my arms wrapped around it like I was giving it a hug. For almost an hour Loc and I sat in the car mourning our homie. Time had seemed to stop as if we pushed pause on a remote. The two of us were stuck in a gruesome nightmare that wouldn't move forward but we wished like hell we could rewind. After finally snapping out of our moment of depression we tried pulling ourselves together while heading to the hood to announce this sad misfortune to our loved ones.

Chapter Twelve

Shot five times and now he's gone. This shit is crazy. Now today we gotta tell his moms he didn't make it. In all the years we been knowin' Baby Cash none of us had ever seen her face. Her voice was heard on the other end of the phone on numerous occasions but that's it. Every blue moon she would call to check on him and in the same breath ask for some money to pay rent, bills, or some other shit. It was this that caused me to dislike her but still in all she is his mother and deserved to know he had passed away. Loc decided he'd be the one to tell her. He dialed her up.

"Hello. Hey Dontrell! What you got for me?" his mother spoke into the phone after seeing Cash's number on the caller id screen

"This isn't Dontrell ma'am. This is his big homeboy."

"Well what you want?"

"Umm..."

"What? He in jail or somethin'."

"Umm I don't know exactly how to tell u this but... Dontrell is dead. He was killed last night. I'm sorry to...."

"Well where is all his money at? Somebody 'bout to bring it to me?" she asked cutting Loc off in the middle of his sentence.

Loc couldn't believe his ears. Holding the receiver in front of his face he looked at the phone then put it back to his ear. Cash's mom was still talking.

"I hope you wasn't callin' me foe no money 'cause I ain't got none and..." The dial tone met her ear. Loc was now fuming with anger.

"Fuck that bitch! She didn't give a fuck about my nigga."

"What happened?" I asked puzzled by his statement.

"That bitch worried about his money and ain't said shit in response to him being dead."

"I told y'all."

"I shoulda asked where she lived and went over there to smoke that bitch," he said seriously.

"I already knew what her ass was about. That's why I didn't like her. Don't trip though, I got enough to pay for the funeral. My nigga worked for me and all that. That's the least I could do. Shit, he would have done it for me."

"Fuck that! I got this. You worry about takin' care of Mai and yo' sisters. I don't got no responsibilities so I'll pay for it. All I'mma do is gamble wit' the shit anyway."

"You sure? I mean, it's not a problem. Even if we just go half or somethin'.

"KeKe!" he said grabbin' me by both shoulders, "I got it. Stop tryin' to do everything alone and let somebody else take care of shit sometimes."

"Okay but if you need me you better call me."

Loc was right. I did need to loosen up a bit and let people help me out sometimes but I been on my own so long I'm not sure I know how. Twelve years of doin' shit on ya own and holdin' down the fam is a long time. It was human nature by now. Not to mention all the people that disappointed me in my life. I could always count on me so why set myself up by tryin' to count on someone else? To me, when people just suddenly come into my life, it's a hidden agenda behind it. By no means was I gonna give anybody the ability to brag about what they did for me or mines. The ones that did, told a half ass story because they were fucked outta their cash and didn't want the world to know. See it's easier for them to say, "Oh I use to fuck that bitch. I'm the reason she got that car." When said that way they appear to be the man and at the same time lower your value to the people listening. The real story, however, is they got a chance to hit but to get the pussy they had to buy me that car. But like I always say to each they own. I didn't care what version they told people cause behind their lies always stood the truth and I was known for keepin' it real.

~$~

Baby Cash's death had everyone on edge. The hood was now labeled the killin' zone. Everyday claimed another life and marked the day that another mother was left to mourn. With all the anger and hostility, even friends began to fall apart. Though no fist were thrown, their words alone, pierced through their hearts like a sword. When the situation became unbearable all hell broke loose.

"I came to get my son money!" an unfamiliar woman said after exiting her 59 Chevy, swiftly approaching the crowd of homies standing in the yard.

"Who is this bitch Cuz?" G Moe asked pullin' his blower out of his waistline.

"Hold up Cuz, I think that's Baby Cash moms," Loc said using his arm to prevent G Moe from takin' aim at the strange woman.

"Are you Baby, I mean, Dontrell's mom?" G Moe asked curiously.

By now, all the homies knew of Loc's animosity toward the woman an if this was, in fact her, Loc was liable to smoke her ass on the spot.

"I sure am. Now who got my son money 'cause I want it. My baby had money out here and now that he's gone it's mine.

Everyone just stood there in silence looking at the woman like she was crazy. Obviously frustrated by their lack of response she yelled, "Hurry up! I got shit to do."

"No the fuck she didn't!" Shell yelled as she made way to the lady's immediate presence and made her presence felt. The whole crowd moved out the way knowin' full well what Shell was about to do. "You beta get yo' fat ass up outta here wit that bullshit foe I beat yo' ass. If anybody gon' get some money it's gon' be me."

"Bullshit!" the lady spat back. "That's my son and..." Before she could finish her sentence Shell had boop-bopped the bitch upside the head.

"Fuck that bitch up moms. Hahaha. You filthy bitch," Loc instigated as the fight went to the next level. The woman never knew what hit her but once the blows started comin' they never stopped. Shell gave it to her live and slept her ass when it was all said and done. The homies were laughing and shakin' hands lovin' every minute of this little episode.

"Aye, I knew moms was gone sleep that bitch. Hahaha! That shit was funny," G Moe laughed as he spoke to no one in particular while standing in the yard.

"That's what her ass get, comin' ova here wit' that bullshit," Loc responded looking at the strange lady lying on the grass completely distraught.

"That's *my* muthafuckin' son, Cuz. He live wit *me* for the past three years. Ain't nobody just gon' pop up thinkin' they runnin' shit ova here. Hell naw!" Shell was mad and now that she was on, it wasn't no turnin' her off. "Get this bitch up outta my yard Cuz. And who else in this muthafuckin' car," she asked opening the passenger door of the car.

Loc headed over to stop her, "Moms! Moms! Don't trip moms, it's cool," he said chuckling and giving her a hug. Shell still didn't calm down and was tryin to break away from Loc's hold.

"Moms look, here goes ten dolla's. Go get you and pops some beer, we got this." And just like that, Shell calmed down, grabbed the money, and said, "Good lookin' out Cuz." Without another word she was gone down the street, throwin' up the "G" as she headed to get her drank.

~$~

The funeral for Baby Cash had come and went, leaving behind a bittersweet feeling amongst the hood. Shit was very different for a while and because of that, along with the pain in my heart, I tried desperately to stay away. Unable to really communicate well with others I stayed in the house and mourned my lost. Matt was gone wit' the wind as usual, never even putting forth the effort to console me. I guess everyone knew how hard I was taking it because no one bothered to show up or call, avoiding any altercations this episode could cause. While lying across my bed lost in my thoughts the phone rang.

"Yeah. Talk."

"Hi beautiful! Why the sad voice? Is everything okay?"

"Not even close but thanks for asking."

"Well I'm back if you wanna talk."

"I don't know D. I probably should just stay to myself."

"Aw come on. You know I'll make you feel better."

D was right. He always made me feel better. His warm embrace was enough to wipe away the worst of my worries. He and I were off to a really good start so I wasn't about to jeopardize that.

BRIDGE 2 DESTRUCTION

"I know you would D," I said wit a slight smile on my face, "but honestly I don't think now is a good time. I'll call you tomorrow or something."

"That bad huh? Well, whenever you need me I'm here."

"Thanks D, bye."

"Bye beautiful."

Now why couldn't that have been Matt? Why? All I'm askin is for him to play his position, the same way I play mines. But noooo... He's been so sprung on the streets he probably don't even realize he has a position at home.

Hours went by and my mind went back and forth about the things heaviest on me at the moment, Baby Cash and D. while I found myself drowning in misery from the pain and hurt I felt in my heart, I spontaneously bore a smile from the joyous thoughts in my head from D.

For days I went through this emotional rollercoaster. I went from happy to sad, from angry to glad, and finally from stressed to content. No one should have to experience a life like this but this was the hand I was dealt so I was gonna play the shit outta the cards I had because throwin' it all in wasn't an option. When I finally regained enough of my sanity to try and get out the house, D was the first person I called to spend some time with. If I was gonna step out this house at least I can go where I'm guaranteed happiness.

When I called his phone he was more than happy to hear from me. Our plan was to meet for lunch and a movie. That was cool, especially since I was in the comfortable mood. I didn't feel like getting all super fly. A simple Aeropostale sweat suit and and some Nike canvas was good enough for me. Add a nice handbag and my signature Gucci shades and I was on point. Within minutes I was out the house headed down the 110 freeway. The wind blew through my hair sending it dancing softly in the air. The traffic was moving at a steady pace allowing me the freedom to maneuver as I pleased. The dj on the radio was doin' his thang, keepin' me rockin' and swayin' to the hip hop beats. When I finally reached the café D stood there looking at me with a smile on his face. His eyes told a story of complete satisfaction and I loved seeing him like that.

Maybe because I knew it was truly genuine and not just a heat of the moment reaction. We've been dating for quite some time and hadn't exchanged any type of intimacy; not even a tongue kiss. As good as he's lookin' today though, I just might give 'em that. Shit if he play his cards right I might even consider giving him some na-na.

Over lunch we discussed everything from what's been goin' on in our lives to what we were gonna do throughout the day. I laughed more than I had in a long time and really enjoyed being out with him. The movie theater we went to was right across the way so we walked hand in hand sharing our feelings for each other. Just when we thought our plans were working out cool, the movie we wanted to see was sold out. It was kind of disappointing because I anticipated lying on his shoulder while he held me in his arms. Damn! But as always he had a backup plan.

"Don't worry sweetheart, we can do something else. If you have time I can take you somewhere nice."

"Is it worth my time?" I asked playfully.

"Everything I do is worth your time, you know that."

"Well lead the way."

Once to the car, he popped in that Eryka Badu and I instantly felt like I was in heaven. The vibe was the business and all I could do was display this million dolla smile the streets caused me to hide. As if that wasn't enough, my eyes were soon met with a view that was romantic and to die for. He had taken me to the Marina and led the way to one of the most beautiful yacht's I'd ever seen. Holding my hand as I stepped on board, he looked into my eyes and said, "Surprise." No words were needed to explain what I felt at that moment. My smile, my sudden display of affection, and my eyes told him that this was special to me.

"Go downstairs and put on that bathing suit. I think I got your size right."

"Bathing suit? Oh so this was already in your plans."

"Not for today but yeah. My plan was to bring you this weekend after you dropped by the house."

BRIDGE 2 DESTRUCTION

Smiling to myself, I made my way to change. The Ed Hardy bikini fit me perfectly. When I reached the upper deck, I noticed we were out far into the water and he was nowhere in sight so I decided to relax until he came back.

Sitting on deck had me in another world. The water was calm, the breeze was moist, and everything seemed to be just right. When he appeared from the mini bar which was located on the lower deck, he possessed two glasses of champagne and some exotic fruits. Slowly, he slid up behind me and planted a kiss on the nape of my neck that sent my pussy into overdrive causing a tingling sensation. For the first time in my life I wanted to make love and without any kind of hidden agenda. I wanted to explore his body and allow him to explore mines. And to my surprise he did just that. After feeding me fruit and sipping champagne he lied me down on the deck and kissed me in my most intimate places. Champagne trickled down my breast as he softly sucked on my nipples. His hands caressed my thighs sending chills up my spine and I opened them for him to lie inside. Kissing and rubbing was all that we did but his tongue alone caused me to climax just as much as I would have had we actually had sex. Clearly

D was nothin' like the rest and even without intercourse he had proven to be the best. He handled me with so much care, delicately touching my body and softly but tenderly kissing my feet. All that this man did said he was a perfect match for me and it's my past experiences won't allow me to fall for him completely. There was no drama, there were no games, and he always did everything he said he would do. Sex wasn't the basis of a relationship with me nor was the money or anything else I could bring to the table. He wanted me and adored me for nothing more and nothing less than me.

After that sexual escapade, I felt very nice.

"I really want you to know how special you are to me. I know you've been through a number of things but if you let me, I promise I got you from here. All I need is for you to be happy and I'll do the rest," he said kneeled down in front of me.

"D, I would love to spend my life with you but I don't wanna bring the mess in my life to yours."

"I'm a grown man Shawn I can handle it."

"Can I think about it?"

"Sure," he said brushing his hand through my head, "just don't leave me hangin' not knowin'."

That moment marked the scariest day of my life. I was actually contemplating goin' against everything I ever felt and or believed as far as relationships are concerned. Was this really a good move to make? Is it safe to say he'd never hurt me or betray me? I don't know. What I do know is this was the perfect place to try and figure it out. Overlooking the water, I found myself lost deep in my thoughts. Silence filled the air for the remainder of our trip but, it was a sensual silence that had us marinating in each other's company.

~$~

When I reached the house everyone was outside scattered all throughout the yard holding expressions of anger and sadness. The atmosphere was filled with so much aggression I had no idea what was about to happen and I wasn't sure if I even wanted to know. On the other hand though, I was very curious. Jumping outta the car with nothing but confusion written all over my face, one of the homies hurried toward me anxious to fill me in on the details.

Before he could utter a word Bo stepped out from the crowd and approached me while sayin', "Ay KeKe, you just the person I been lookin' for. Kai in jail Cuz. The team hit this muthafucka today and found a blower. I called your phone but you didn't answer."

"What you mean they took Kai? Took her for what," I asked confused.

"They came to get her on a 187 and just so happen to find a blower. I don't know what's about to happen. Man this shit is crazy. My girl ain't neva been to jail before and a 187 shhh." Bo couldn't believe what was happening. It was all too far-fetched for him. He was definitely gonna get to the bottom of this.

"That ain't even Kai's get down my nigga," I said tryin' to cover for her but in truth I knew full well what he was referring to. Kai and I dreaded this day for a long time coming and now I have to make sure I do something to get her outta this situation.

"Shit if they was comin' to get anybody it shoulda been KeKe's crazy ass. Y'all know her ass been wildin' for a long time," one of the homies said while conversing with some of the other homies from the block.

When I approached them those were the only words I heard and it had me wonderin', who had been wildin' for a long time? "Who y'all talkin' about," I asked for some type of clarity. Bo repeated the conversation and as if I couldn't feel any lower, the whole situation left me feelin' like I was the one to blame. Truthfully I felt a little better when I was sittin behind them bars instead of her. I never wanted this for any of my sisters. I guess Trials and tribulations is my specialty 'cause shit happens to me around the clock and every time it does I find a way to fix it and pull it all back together again. *Fuck this*, I thought to myself. *I'm about to smoke me a blunt. It worked before, it has to work again.*

Here I am sittin' by this phone like I'm waitin' on a million dolla phone call and Kai's ass still ain't called. I'm tired of pacing back and forth and callin' everybody I can think of to see if they heard from her. I wanted to believe she was okay with every part of my being but I know how it feels to sit behind them bars, I know the games and the lies the police play, just like I know Kai ain't ready to deal with those types of situations. I witnessed the depression this situation sent her through and I just don't want her to say or do anything that's gonna incriminate herself.

Harmony and Mai came running into the living room arguing about what they had said to one another in the room. Neither one of them knew of the frustration I was dealing with at the time, needless to say the bickering made me snap almost immediately. Soon as I did Mai started laughing, "Haha I told you my mama don't wanna hear that."

"But Aunt T, Mai said my mama ain't never comin' home cause Bo don't got no money to go get her."

"Mai! Did you say that?" when I jumped up off of that couch Mai thought twice about answering me but knew she better unless I was really gonna beat her ass. "Yes ma'am. But…."

Before she could say another word I had knocked fire from her ass. "You bet not eva let me find out you talkin' to yo cousin like that. You don't know what nobody got so keep yo mouth closed. You worry 'bout what money you don't got and please know I'm not givin' you shit since that's how you treat yo family."

Kai was both hurt and embarrassed. She expected me to side with her or maybe just figured I wouldn't listen to it at all but she was sadly mistaking. One thing I don't do is tolerate family treating family any less than they would treat a muthafucka off the streets.

Chapter Thirteen

"Hey Shawn!" D said all excited into the phone.

"What's up?"

"Come by the house today. I got somethin' special planned for you."

"Oh you doin' some special shit again? What could it possibly be this time?"

"I think it's time you met my family and some of my boys from around the way."

BRIDGE 2 DESTRUCTION

"Aw shit! I'm meeting family and shit now? Watch out haters cause ya girl gettin' it in."

"Hahaha bye Silly. Be here by eight."

"Alright."

I can't wait to meet the family, I thought to myself running to the closet to find some of my flyest gear. With my hair on point and nails freshly manicured, when I finished getting' ready I looked like a million bucks. A 360 degree turn displayed curves in all the right places and just enough bling to make a short and sweet statement. A couple of dabs of Pink Sugar perfume by Aquolina left me smelling pleasantly sensual. Just what I needed to leave a lasting impression.

Pulling through the gate I checked myself in the mirror one last time. The long horseshoe-shaped driveway was full of nice cars. Mines fit perfectly. Jumping out of my Lexus SC430 wit the retractable top, all eyes were on me as I walked through the door. The first to greet me, and right on cue, was D.

"Shawn! I'm glad you made it," before landing a soft firm kiss on my lips, "You lookin' beautiful as always."

"You don't look too bad yourself," I said lookin' at him in his chocolate linen short set with his Louis Vuitton shoes. I could see we thought just alike when it came to accessorizing cause all he bore was simple chain, a diamond studded earring, and a pinky ring that spoke volumes.

"Let me introduce you to my moms," he said holding my hand leading the way through the crowd and out the patio door. "Mom!"

With five different women sitting there, it wasn't clear to me who he was referring to. The lady I least expected it to be responded, "What boy?" Her beauty was far past gorgeous and she was the younger looking of the bunch.

"I want you to meet my better half. Shawn this my mama Cassandra. Mama this is Shawn."

We both said "Hi" in unison and she greeted me with a hug before sayin', "It's nice to meet you baby. I don't know what you did to this here son of mines but you keep on doin' it. He's only introduced me to one woman his whole life so meeting you let's know he really adores you."

Still mesmerized by her beauty I just smiled and said, "I hope so."

For a moment all we did was chop it up with different people; family, friends, you name it. Just as I started to enjoy myself I get a strange feeling that someone is watching me. No one stood out or made eye contact with me as I looked around the room. *I don't know. Maybe I'm just trippin'.*

"I'll be right back. I need to use the ladies room," I whispered in his ear to avoid yelling over the loud music.

"Don't stay gone too long."

"Shut up Silly. Hold my drink."

As I made my way to the bathroom D smiled and watched me in awe.

Meanwhile....

"Ay fool, where you been hidin' at? I gotta introduce you to my girl."

"Naw man, I'm cool," Myles said coldly with a look of disapproval on his face.

"What you mean, you cool? You my nigga! You gotta meet shorty, she gone be yo' sister-in-law one day."

For a second, Myles didn't say nothin', just looked into space shakin' his head like, nah. D couldn't understand for life of him what this shit was about. Especially since for almost nine months he was diggin' baby and couldn't wait to meet her judging by their past conversations.

"Get at me my nigga. If you got somethin' to say, say it."

"Now ain't the time, bro."

"Now is the perfect time. Follow me out by the pool so we can talk."

Standing by the pool Myles began to speak his peace. "Remember I told you about us spendin' Sunday nights on the Shaw?"

"Yeah, what about it?"

"The bitch you wit....," Myles gave D a quick rundown on what happened that painful night. D stood with his arms crossed taking in the whole story but still wasn't convinced that what Myles proposed was true.

"That's that bitch Ocho, I'm tellin' you," Myles said ready to flip into action.

"Are you sure man? I think you just trippin' homie cause baby don't get down like that. She's good folks."

"This ain't no coincidence my nigga. She look like the bitch and shaped like the bitch."

"But you said it yo 'self, Myles, the woman you talkin' about had an accent and had brown and blonde hair. Plus Shawn has dimples. You didn't say nothin' about ole girl havin' any."

"Ay fool, where you been hidin' at? I gotta introduce you to my girl."

"Naw man, I'm cool," Myles said coldly with a look of disapproval on his face.

"What you mean, you cool? You my nigga! You gotta meet shorty, she gone be yo' sister-in-law one day."

For a second, Myles didn't say nothin', just looked into space shakin' his head like, nah. D couldn't understand for life of him what this shit was about. Especially since for almost nine months he was diggin' baby and couldn't wait to meet her judging by their past conversations.

"Get at me my nigga. If you got somethin' to say, say it."

"Now ain't the time, bro."

"Now is the perfect time. Follow me out by the pool so we can talk."

Standing by the pool Myles began to speak his peace. "Remember I told you about us spendin' Sunday nights on the Shaw?"

"Yeah, what about it?"

"The bitch you wit....," Myles gave D a quick rundown on what happened that painful night. D stood with his arms crossed taking in the whole story but still wasn't convinced that what Myles proposed was true.

"That's that bitch Ocho, I'm tellin' you," Myles said ready to flip into action.

"Are you sure man? I think you just trippin' homie cause baby don't get down like that. She's good folks."

"This ain't no coincidence my nigga. She look like the bitch and shaped like the bitch."

"But you said it yo 'self, Myles, the woman you talkin' about had an accent and had brown and blonde hair. Plus Shawn has dimples. You didn't say nothin' about ole girl havin' any."

"You know what, I'mma leave it alone. Watch that bitch man, 'cause I know I'm right."

A firm handshake was exchanged accompanied by a quick shoulder to shoulder hug and Myles left the gathering upset that his lifelong friend, for the first time in their life, didn't trust his judgment.

~$~

I came out of the restroom only to find D no longer stood there. My effort to find him was constantly sidetracked by questions and comments from family and friends. Ten minutes later, when I finally spotted him across the way, his demeanor caught me by surprise. He looked upset like something terrible had happened. What was once smiles and genuine excitement was now a ball of confusion causing his attempts to pretend everything was fine, to be evident.

"What's wrong?"

He shook it off, displaying a phony smile and said, "Nothin.. nothing… don't even worry about it." We exchanged a kiss and just like that everything went back to the way it was prior to me leaving the room.

BRIDGE 2 DESTRUCTION

The night for me, overall, was like a dream come true. I was not only on cloud nine with this man but I was introduced to and accepted by his family and friends. This was it. I was finally where I needed to be, so first thing in the morning I'm gonna cut all these loose strings.

Chapter Fourteen

"Bye Matt! I'm leaving. When you get this message you might wanna come straight home so the door won't be unlocked all day. I hope the streets were worth it my nig, *MOVIN!*"

When the call ended I gave the house one last look and headed out the door, bags in tow. While the wooden door was secure, the bar door was just pushed close. The dead bolt lock prevented me from locking it since I left behind the keys and everything else he had ever given me; the car, the clothes, jewelry, and the money. No parts of him were going with me. I had moved on to embrace the new me.

Moving took a couple of trips because I had to make sure I had all of Mai's things and at the same time move both of my cars. Things were a whole lot different from the average breakups. There wasn't any arguing, questioning, hostility, or fighting. Shit, I didn't even go off on his answering machine. I calmly and nicely stated my claim and left. Unfortunately that wasn't good enough. Two hours after I had finished my move and laid back on my mom's couch to relax, my phone rang.

"Talk."

"What the fuck you mean talk? So you gone? Bitch I gave you everything you got. I'll come take all that shit."

Still remaining calm I replied, "You must not be home yet," and smiled. "And why you getting' at me all foul? I didn't get off on you."

"I'm here now. Why is my muthafuckin' door unlocked? And where is my keys?"

"The wooden door *is* locked and your keys are on the living room table."

As Matt walked in the house he was shocked to find the house in top notch condition and the keys on the table just as I promised. Unable to just accept it and let it go that easily, he went off some more. "Oh so you done spent all a nigga money and now you gone? You ain't shit!"

"If you go in the room you will see in your top drawer there's about $8000. The jewelry is on the dresser for you to do what you want and the car is parked in the back. I don't need your money or nothin' else you got. Give it to the next bitch; I'm good. Have a nice life. Loved ya! Hahaha."

My choice of words, along with his own visual confirmation, did more damage than I could have imagined. He was use to feelin' like he was the man and I needed him. Now he had to accept the real truth; a real bitch don't *need* a nigga she just *wants* one. While he thought he was the player in this game, my first, last, and only move proved that I played this game better than he ever will.

~$~

My mother and father accepted me in their home, this time, with open arms. It was like a long awaited reunion they had wanted to happen. I still wasn't all that close with my dad but even in the midst of all that was goin' on I could see a change in him. I spent a lot of time wondering what had changed and then it hit me. He was sober. A smile spread across my face. That day, for the first time, I think I understood why my mother stayed with him. All of the times I seen him he was a drunken monster, rarely around long enough to see him sober. My mother on the other hand had seen everything since she was the young age of thirteen. When sober, he was a gentleman, funny, loving, and respectful at all times. Because of that I was happy for them.

"Damn KeKe, you lookin' fly," Tray told me while giving me a hug. "So we about to live it up today?"

"Yeah. You know me. I ain't 'bout to just sit at home on my C-day."

Everyone had made their store runs and shit so we got ready to load up. Joe's Crab Shack was screamin' my name and I was ready to answer its call. Lookin' fly ass shit, but not really in my grown woman mood, I decided to drive my I-ROC. As soon as I pressed the button to fire it up this nigga Matt hit the corner and jumped out on me.

"Fuck you bitch!" was all he yelled before commencing to fuck my car up. Everything he could think of doing he did, including jumping on the roof, slightly caving it in.

"Somebody better get this nigga, Cuz," I spat. But nobody wanted to get involved. "Why you come ova here fuckin' wit' me and my shit? I didn't do that hoe shit to you and neva have."

"So what! Fuck all this shit!"

Laughing for a second from this unbelievable episode, I calmly shook my head and stated my claim. "Cuz, you a hater. You wanted them bitches and these streets, I gave you that. I didn't question you, nag you, or none of that. I just calmly left and gave you all yo' shit back. What's the problem?"

"Bitch you the problem," he said and discarded a super soaker spraying me down along with the inside of my car. The homies stood around looking in disbelief.

"Aw Cuz, that's fucked up," one of them said. This nigga was tryin' super hard to ruin my day and since I knew his intention, it didn't work. Instead I laughed at his ass and clowned him for acting like a female.

"You done? I'm still goin' out wet and all."

While standing in front of him I clipped my hair up which was now curly, popped my trunk to put on a t-shirt, blew him a kiss, and asked, "you wanna go," as I put the car in gear.

"Let's move y'all! This nigga ain't stop shit." In unison we sped off down the street, me leading the pact, throwin' up the 'G'. The whole situation low key pissed me off but I wasn't about to let it show. My day was gonna crack just as I planned. Misery loves company and that company ain't neva been me.

Just like I planned, my day went well and the smoke-out afterwards put the icing on the cake. Every crip on the east side was in attendance and of course, that caused problems. The loud music along with over fifty niggas chanting, 'MOVIN'... was a clear invitation for the police to come shut us down. When they arrived they bought the whole force with 'em and made all of us disburse. Even with the early ending, my day was the business and kept people talkin' for days on in.

Chapter Fifteen

The next day, not only was it hot enough to cook on the concrete but the day came with some mo' drama. And so did the next day, and the next day, and the day after that. Matt was on a mission to make my life as miserable as possible but I shined it on like it was nothing. The more I ignored his childish antics the wilder his tantrums became. Everyday something or someone caught in the cross fire was destroyed. It happened like that all the way up until I snapped. While standing on the sidewalk of the block in which we lived I heard a loud scream from down the street. "KeKe watch out, he got a gun!"

I have the ability to deal wit a lot of things but a gun pointed at me wasn't one of 'em. Hearing those disturbing words caused me to flip into defense mode. So with the swiftness of a cheetah, I ran to my car retrieving both my .380 and glock 17. My natural reflexes caused me to pull mines and although my trigger fingers were itchin', I didn't wanna kill him. As he approached me I noticed his gun was at his side so I lowered mines and waited patiently for him to make the wrong move. Standing face to face with him was like challenging a lion. But I had too much heart and not enough sense to back down.

"Is this what you came for Matt? Are you sure you want this? If not, I suggest you leave 'cause I'm really ready and willing to give it to you."

The look in his eyes spoke volumes. He was workin' wit' feelins and had just did some dumb shit but my willingness to go against him at all cost destroyed his ego and damaged his heart. Instead of takin' things to the next level, he stood silently looking in my eyes, allowing me to see his pain before he turned and walked away. I felt bad for him but at the same time this is what he wanted and it was time for me to give it to him. It was either stand for somethin' or fall for any and everything. Besides, there was someone who wanted to be in my life so why stay with the person whom held no interest?

~$~

Five months of dating and D and I were inseparable. Whenever time permitted us to, we were together, living it up and fallin' deeper and deeper in love. He was now comfortable enough with me to allow me complete access into his world. I had keys to the house, access to two trap houses, and an all access pass to any and everywhere he was. While our relationship continued to get better and better, his friendship with Myles had gotten worse. In the past five months I can only recall seeing Myles once, which was disturbing because I use to hear about him every day. Whenever I asked D about him he would respond, "He cool," and leave it at that. Something wasn't right though and I knew it.

"When will I get to meet him face to face?" I asked him out of curiosity.

"Soon babe," he lied sounding dry and very unsure. With the King Day Parade approaching there was no doubt I would see him and when I did I was gonna get down to the bottom of this. I've never been the one to pretend or act like things were cool when they clearly weren't, so why start now?

~$~

Today is beautiful. The sun is shining brightly, the breeze is cool but soft, and the airs aroma is sweet. Dressed in a new Christian Audiger tank top with some tight fitted jeans complimented by some Ed Hardy shades, I jumped in my I ROC and hit the highway to pick up Mai from Kai's house. When I arrived at the house Mai walked out looking just as cute as ever.

"Hey Mama!"

"Hey lil lady. What you doin' dressed like me," I asked her playfully.

She laughed for a minute and then replied, "I'm a princess I suppose to be cute. Just like my momma," and sat her little purse on the seat to buckle her seatbelt.

"Excuse me prin-cess."

I loved to see my baby mimic me and show how confident she was with herself. It reminded me of how I was before I lost my innocence. My granny always treated me like and molded me into a lady. Therefore, I did the same with Mai. Everything instilled in me that was positive or even sentimental as a child, I promised to instill in my children, even if it took my last breath. It was those things that kept me grounded and determined whether I made it or drowned with the rest of the low life's surrounding me. It was those very things that kept me from being that fast ass little girl being manipulated by the wolves that were eagerly waiting to attack me in the streets. I may have made some fucked up decisions but I was a woman about my shit. I was able to be that strong stand up bitch that I needed to be and determined how and when things would happen. Thinking about it pisses me off but at the same time it brings a smile to my face because I handled my business. My family was cool, I was cool, and I never had to ask or beg anybody for shit. It was grown ass women around me every day that couldn't hold shit down like I did and I was a kid. Some of them were more into these nigga than they were their own children while others were just flat out tryin' to keep up wit the Jones's, buyin' everything they could to perpetrate like they had it like that while their kids were at home wit the lights about to get cut off and no food in the refrigerator to eat.

Snapping out of my daze, I looked over and caught Mai singing into her fist like it was a microphone. "Get it baby!" I said to her like she was the best in the music industry.

"Aw mommie! You messed me up dang," she said blushing and covering her face.

"How I mess you up?"

"'Cause. I don't like when you be all pumped up and lookin' at me."

"Oh. My bad. Well what am I supposed to do then?"

"Just listen."

"Okay."

As soon as I pretended to be occupied and appeared as though I wasn't paying any attention to her, she sprung back into action. I giggled inside at her little performance but I must say that my baby had a voice on her. Pulling up into the mall parking lot with the music bumpin' and Mai singin' all eyes were on me. Everybody seemed to be mesmerized by my whip. I was used to it at this point though. One group of bitches was on me tough as I pulled in and I couldn't wait to shut their asses down. Nine times outta ten they're some hatters anyway. As I sat waiting for the car aside me to pull out of its parking stall I heard one of the girls say, "Girl I bet that's her nigga car, while she all up here flossin' like she the shit." I laughed to myself then politely burst their bubble. "Um excuse me! You might wanna check out this back window," I said with a smile.

As they passed my car and were able to see the window, all their asses felt dumb and turned their nose up as they read, "BITCH IT'S MINES" on the back window. Hahaha I laughed to myself as I enjoyed another moment of shittin' on yet another hater. When I turned to focus my attention back on the stall I was waiting for another woman had swooped in and took it. The crowd of girls laughed hysterically. "That's what her ass get," one of them spat. I was pissed. No sooner than they started laughing their smiles were turned upside down when I emerged from the car fly ass hell but ignorant as a muthafucka. "I know you betta move yo' shit. You seen me wit' my blinker on about to park right here."

"I'm not movin' nothin'," the lady said definitely and began rollin' her windows up. *No this bitch didn't*, I thought to myself. Before the drivers window could go all the way up I was at her car ready to whoop her ass.

"Oh god, not again," Mai said putting her hand over her face shaking her head.

"Bitch I swear to god if you don't move this peace of shit outta my way I'm gonna stump a mud hole in yo' ass." Seeing I was far from kidding the lady put her car in reverse to back out. But not before getting smart. As I got back into my car she leaned out the window, "Next time act like you want the muthafucka then!" she said.

"Wha... Hold on! What this bitch just say? Gimme somethin'Mai, gimme somethin'. Hurry up!" Mai not wanting to see anything happen said,

BRIDGE 2 DESTRUCTION

"Mamaaaaaa! Don't..." but it was already too late. I had grabbed my bottle of soda out of the cup holder and hummed that muthafucka right at her window. Soda was now splattered on her car as the bottle exploded from the impact from the car. "Aw hell naw," the woman said throwing her car into park as if she was about to jump out or somethin'. Soon as I parked I jumped out and said, "Do something bitch. I want you to. Hurry up and do somethin'," The lady looked at me like I had completely lost my damn mind and quickly threw her car in gear then pulled out of the parking lot at top speed. *Oh stupid bitch*, I thought to myself as I walked back toward the car leanin' in to grab my keys out of the ignition. "I can't even come to the mall without stupid ass people playin' wit' me. I mean damn, is drama gonna follow me everywhere I go? Come on baby let's go get our shop on."

At this point Mai doesn't even wanna go in the mall. She was embarrassed and fed up with the way her mom just flipped out on people all of the time. Somethin' had to give. *Is she crazy*, Mai thought to herself. "Mama I think you need to go to the doctor."

"What you mean go to the doctor? For what?"

"Cause you need some medicine."

"Girl please! Ain't nothing wrong wit' me," I said throwing my hand out in her direction as if she were trippin'.

"No, for real mama. You be gettin' real mad all the time."

"That's because somebody always doin' somethin' to make me mad. I don't just get mad for nothing. Now come on before I change my mind."

The car door slammed shut and I hit the alarm to ensure we'd still have a car once we got back to the parking lot. Before we could enter the mall Mai stopped in her tracks, looked at me, and said, "Mommie please don't fight okay." The look upon her face was sad yet serious and it bothered me more than ever. "Baby I'm not gonna fight. We are gonna go in this mall and shop till we drop, grab us some Hot Dog on a Stick, and go home." With those few words Mai's face lit up with excitement and she was back to her normal, happy self. "And don't forget the cookies Mommie!"

"Ha ha ha. And we won't forget the cookies."

BRIDGE 2 DESTRUCTION

The mall was packed like church on Easter Sunday. Everybody and their grandma were in here today and the food court was where most of the business was. Squeezing through the crowd of individuals mingling in the walkway of the food court irritated the shit outta me. I wanted so badly to ask them if there was a problem with moving over to allow us space to walk through. One look at Mai was enough to get me to keep my mouth shut. I had just promised my baby I wouldn't be in here getting' mad or fightin', so I kept my word and stood in front of the disrespectful crowd of individuals and said excuse me at least two times. Nothin' happened! They completely ignored me. "Ex-cuse me!" I said one last time with emphasis.

Surprisingly not, the crowd shifted separate ways creating a path and one of the men gave me a look of surprise before saying, "Damn lil mama, our bad." *You goddamn right ya'lls bad*, is what I wanted to say to his raggedy ass but because I'm a woman of my word I smiled and said, "That's okay!" while holding my daughter's hand leading her to the escalator. Mai's smile was bigger than ever, maybe because she was proud of me for simply being cordial for a change.

Our first stop was children's place, Mai's second most favorite store in the world. From there we hit Kid's Footlocker. We entered and exited almost every store the mall had to accommodate little girls. Needless to say our trip to the food court before we left was a difficult one. Bags were swinging, dangling, and falling all over the place. Mai thought it was quite funny while I, on the other hand, found it a bit uncomfortable. But hey, this day was for my baby and everything she wanted to do we were gonna do.

"Hi may I take your order," the young lady wearing a multi-colored, stripped outfit with the hat to match asked.

"I want a corn dog, some French fries, and a red juice," Mai responded. "And give my mommie one too." The cashier laughed and placed the two orders just as Mai said and moved on to the next customer.

"Thanks for ordering my food Princess."

"You're welcome," she said smiling and full of energy.

Times like these are the reason I do what I do. The smile on Mai's face was worth far more than a million dollars. If the little things can satisfy my baby to this extent then the big things would be like a dream come true and she would definitely appreciate it. After the mall we hit a movie and finally went home. After our baths Mai lay upon my chest and fell asleep.

Chapter Sixteen

You know what? I miss my boo. Today I think I'll surprise him at the café for lunch. Yeah, that's exactly what I'm gonna do, I thought to myself as I lay comfortably on the couch watching lifetime. The movie I was watching was just about over so after that I'll take a shower so I can be sure to catch him before he leaves. D was always about business but was sure to put himself and his family before it all. I think that's what I like the most about him. He knew how to separate the two. Though most men would put his money before anything, D knew the importance of family. Ten deals could cross his table and none of them would be touched until after he completed the task he had goin' with his loved ones. If your money or your business wasn't good enough for tomorrow then fuck you and he wasn't losin' no sleep over it.

"So what's up handsome," I asked while giving him a warm hug followed by a soft kiss on the lips.

"Damn baby! I'm better now. When a beautiful black queen comes up to a brotha like me with kiss and a hug, smellin' all good and shit, a nigga like me gotta be doin' good."

"Shut up Silly," I said playfully hitting him in the chest. "I missed you."

"Is that right? Well I'm glad you came to see me because I missed you too."

"Aw hell naw D!" someone yelled aggressively from the door of the café. "This shit ain't cool homie. It's one thing when *you* choose to fuck wit' her but it's a whole 'nother ball game when you bring this shit around me," Myles stated.

"Hold up Myles. Don't..." For a few seconds I was clueless as to what was goin' on. Then it hit me. They talkin' bout me and this nigga obviously don't like me. So when I interrupted D's attempted response I was kinda heated.

"No babe, you hold on! What the hell is this all about?"

"What you think it's about? Bitch this shit is about you."

"Bitch? Nigga first of all watch who you talkin' to. You don't even know me while you callin' me outta my fuckin' name."

"I know yo' snake ass and just like I said, *Bitch* you need to get the fuck from 'round me."

D was tryin' hard to hold me and keep me from approachin' his disrespectful friend. At the same time he kept signaling for Myles to shut this bullshit down. No matter what he said or did Myles and I both continued to express our anger towards each other.

"Oh and now I'm a snake? Where the fuck you know me from? Tell me that, huh?"

"I'm not about to keep goin' back and forth with you."

"No! Tell me where the fuck you know me from."

"You know me bitch. Yo' snake ass met my nigga on Crenshaw. He went to fuck yo' stankin', rat ass. Fuck! I told my nigga to stay."

When he said that, my mind went into overdrive tryin' to recall who he was talkin' about. While I stood there with my eyes squinted and face frowned up he made a comment that would bring everything to the forefront.

"My nigga got killed tryin' to fuck on yo' stankin' ass."

Those words took my mind straight to the incident he was referring to. As soon as that particular moment was refreshed in my mind giving me a visual of that crazy night, a light bulb came on. His face appeared from my memory bank and I knew exactly who he was. By this time D was standing with his arms crossed evaluating the situation as it unraveled before his eyes. The look on my face must have sent a confirmation message because he looked at me confused awaiting my reply.

"I don't know what you talkin' about," I responded.

"All my niggas will vouch for me D. Let's take her ass to the spot and see how much she remembers then."

"I'm not goin' nowhere."

D looked at me like I had just made the biggest mistake of my life. "So hold up. Myles, my nigga, you sure this her?"

"Man I'm... Fuck this! I'm takin' her to the spot," he said approaching me with his arm stretched out to grab me. And when he did I reached in my purse to grab my boyfriend. If this nigga thought he was about to do anything to me he was sadly mistakin'. But before I could pull my weapon D interjected and said,

"What you doin'? Wait a minute. So this you? You really the bitch that killed my little brother?"

Fire was in his eyes. I've never seen him like this before. Everything he displayed at this very moment scared me. There was nowhere for me to go and nobody here to help me. Common sense said go hard or you're about to die, so that's what I did. I snatched away from D and went for my gun a second time. Only this time, both D and Myles pulled their weapons also and unloaded a ripple of bullets into various parts of my body. The impact of the bullets caused me to drop to the ground after getting off three rounds myself. I couldn't come to grips with what just happened. My legs were sore, my chest was burning and my head along with my clothes were wet. I tried numerous times to get up off the ground but couldn't. With all the strength I had left in my body I slid toward my car tryin' my hardest to escape my attackers. I could hear screaming and a man goin' crazy about losing another loved one. My vision became blurry but I could still see a glare of my surroundings. The male voice got closer and closer and sounded even angrier than before. When he stopped a short distance away from me something shinny caught my attention causing me to raise my gun one last time. This was the weakest I've ever been so squeezing the trigger was extremely hard. Thoughts of my daughter ran through my mind causing my adrenaline to shoot through the roof. There's no way I'm gonna die like this. Not here and not now. My baby needs me right now and I can't let these punk ass niggas take that away from her. Thinking these thoughts would usually re-boost my energy giving me the strength I needed to push through whatever trial I was facing. But this time was different. Thoughts were all I seemed to have left. Two shots fired, from whose gun I have no idea. Certainly it wasn't mine. No sooner than it had, silence filled the air and everything went black.

COMING THIS WINTER

From:

Top Notch

Publishing

THE TREACHEROUS TALE
OF EBONY & IVORY

Not My Sister's Keeper

THE DEBUT NOVEL FROM

Sequaia Reed

www.ingramcontent.com/pod-product-compliance
Lightning Source LLC
LaVergne TN
LVHW051552070426
835507LV00021B/2538